The New York Times

SO-EIL-030

CHANGING PERSPECTIVES

Race Relations

THE NEW YORK TIMES EDITORIAL STAFF

Published in 2019 by New York Times Educational Publishing in association with The Rosen Publishing Group, Inc. 29 East 21st Street, New York, NY 10010

First Edition

The New York Times
Alex Ward: Editorial Director, Book Development
Brenda Hutchings: Senior Photo Editor/Art Buyer
Phyllis Collazo: Photo Rights/Permissions Editor
Heidi Giovine: Administrative Manager

Rosen Publishing
Greg Tucker: Creative Director
Brian Garvey: Art Director
Megan Kellerman: Managing Editor

Cataloging-in-Publication Data
Names: New York Times Company.
Title: Race relations / edited by the New York Times editorial staff.
Description: New York : The New York Times Educational Publishing, 2019. | Series: Changing perspectives | Includes glossary and index.
Identifiers: ISBN 9781642820379 (pbk.) | ISBN 9781642820362 (library bound) | ISBN 9781642820355 (ebook)
Subjects: LCSH: Race relations—Juvenile literature. | Race discrimination—Juvenile literature. |
United States—Race relations—Juvenile literature. | Race discrimination—Juvenile literature.
Classification: LCC HT1521.R334 2019 | DDC 305.8—dc23

Manufactured in the United States of America

On the cover: People gather in protest in Ferguson, Mo., on August 16, 2014; Eric Thayer for the New York Times.

Contents

8   Introduction

CHAPTER 1

From Slavery to Emancipation

10   The Chaplin Case BY THE NEW YORK TIMES

12   The Colored Race BY THE NEW YORK TIMES

15   Arrest of a Fugitive Slave BY THE NEW YORK TIMES

16   An Indian Encounter. BY THE NEW YORK TIMES

18   Letter of the Chinamen to his Excellency, Gov. Bigler.
     BY THE NEW YORK TIMES

25   Douglas vs. Douglass, Settlement of Nebraska
     BY THE NEW YORK TIMES

30   Decision of the Supreme Court in the Dred Scott Case — The
     Position of Slavery in the Constitution. BY THE NEW YORK TIMES

32   Emancipation. President Lincoln's Proclamation.
     THE NEW YORK TIMES

35   The President's Proclamation BY THE NEW YORK TIMES

38   The Consummation! Slavery Forever Dead in the United States.
     BY THE NEW YORK TIMES

40   The South and the Negro Vote. FROM THE CHARLESTON MERCURY

42 The Conduct and Attitude of the Southern Opposition
BY THE NEW YORK TIMES

46 What Next? BY THE NEW YORK TIMES

49 Plain Truths for the Negroes. BY THE NEW YORK TIMES

52 Woman's Rights and the Fashions — A Rebuke from
"Sojourner Truth." BY THE NEW YORK TIMES

53 Louisiana's Separate Car Law. BY THE NEW YORK TIMES

CHAPTER 2

The Promise of Equality

54 Race Problem Conference; Speakers at Montgomery Discuss
Lynching; Extermination of Blacks Said to Be Inevitable
BY THE NEW YORK TIMES

57 Is the Turk a White Man? BY THE NEW YORK TIMES

59 Socialist Advises Negroes to Strike BY THE NEW YORK TIMES

64 Written on the Screen BY THE NEW YORK TIMES

65 A Woman's Protest THE NEW YORK TIMES

66 Negroes Mob Photo Play. BY THE NEW YORK TIMES

67 Bar Negro Women's Vote. BY THE NEW YORK TIMES

68 Better Relations Between Races Sought At a Student
Conference in the South BY THE NEW YORK TIMES

69 New Racial Ideas Taught BY THE NEW YORK TIMES

72 West Coast Moves to Oust Japanese BY LAWRENCE E. DAVIES

73 Upholds Japanese in Citizens' Right BY LAWRENCE E. DAVIES

75 Fifty Years of Crusading for the Negro in America
BY LOMBARD C. JONES

79 How to Prevent Riots THE NEW YORK TIMES

80 Move to Curb Racial Strife BY THE NEW YORK TIMES

82 Housing Plan Sets Tenancy Standards BY THE NEW YORK TIMES

83 Big Negro Colonies Worry West-Coast BY GEORGE STREATOR

85 Texas Fights Bias to Insure Supply of Mexican Labor BY JOHN E. KING

87 'Wetback' Patrol to Be Stepped Up; 500 Officers to Augment Unit
of 256 on Mexico Border to Halt Alien Influx BY THE NEW YORK TIMES

CHAPTER 3

The Civil Rights Era

88 Racial Issues Stirred by Mississippi Killing BY JOHN N. POPHAM

93 Negroes' Boycott Cripples Bus Line BY THE NEW YORK TIMES

95 Militia Sent to Little Rock; School Integration Put Off
BY BENJAMIN FINE

99 Negro Protests Lead to Store Closings BY THE NEW YORK TIMES

100 Negro Rejected at Mississippi U.; U. S. Seeks Writs
BY CLAUDE SITTON

104 Violence in Mississippi Has Roots in Slavery Furor of the 1830's;
Racial Views Are Probably Unshaken BY CLAUDE SITTON

110 Negro Planning Jobless March BY THE NEW YORK TIMES

113 New York's Racial Unrest: Negroes' Anger Mounting
BY LAYHMOND ROBINSON

129 "I Have a Dream" BY JAMES RESTON

133 Birmingham Bomb Kills 4 Negro Girls in Church; Riots Flare;
2 Boys Slain BY CLAUDE SITTON

137 Civil Rights Victory BY THE NEW YORK TIMES

138 Incident at Selma BY THE NEW YORK TIMES

139 Dr. King Deplores 'Long Cold Winter' On the Rights Front
BY THE NEW YORK TIMES

140 The Ghetto Explodes in Another City BY THE NEW YORK TIMES

143 Marriage Curbs by States Scored BY FRED P. GRAHAM

145 Slaying Recalls Series of Deaths That Have Marked Rights Fight
BY SETH S. KING

CHAPTER 4

One Step Forward, Two Steps Back

147 Desegregation Course Charted By Legal Unit After Bus Ruling
BY C. GERALD FRASER

150 Standing Up for Civil Rights BY THE NEW YORK TIMES

151 An 'Aberration' or Police Business as Usual? BY THE NEW YORK TIMES

153 Officer Says Beaten Man Resisted BY SETH MYDANS

154 Los Angeles Policemen Acquitted in Taped Beating BY SETH MYDANS

161 Officers in Bronx Fire 41 Shots, And an Unarmed Man Is Killed
BY MICHAEL COOPER

165 Broader Palette Allows for Subtler Census Portrait BY ERIC SCHMITT

169 U.S. Schools Turn More Segregated, a Study Finds
BY DIANA JEAN SCHEMO

171 Sept. 11 Attack Narrows the Racial Divide BY SOMINI SENGUPTA

176 Obama Elected President as Racial Barrier Falls
BY ADAM NAGOURNEY

182 A Lynching in Brooklyn BY THE NEW YORK TIMES

183 For Puerto Ricans, Sotomayor's Success Stirs Pride
BY DAVID GONZALEZ

187 Deep Tensions Rise to Surface After Ferguson Shooting
BY TANZINA VEGA AND JOHN ELIGON

193 When Will Black Lives Matter in St. Louis? BY NICOLE D. NELSON

196 The Heartbeat of Racism Is Denial BY IBRAM X. KENDI

200 There's Never Been a Native American Congresswoman.
That Could Change in 2018. BY JULIE TURKEWITZ

205 Korematsu, Notorious Supreme Court Ruling on Japanese
Internment, Is Finally Tossed Out BY CHARLIE SAVAGE

209 Glossary
212 Media Literacy Terms
214 Media Literacy Questions
215 Citations
221 Index

Introduction

RACE IS A CONCEPT. Like all concepts, it isn't so much a thing that people encounter in the world and then investigate, describe, discuss and consider when making decisions. Rather, race is largely a social construct. The concept of race is created and reinforced as people talk about it, think about it and act on it. And it is usually used as a tool for members of one group of people to more effectively dominate people from another group. Since race is a social construct, perhaps the best way to learn about it is to track the ways discussions about race have developed and changed over time.

This book is a guide to the discussions about race relations in the United States as they have been covered by The New York Times, from its inception in 1851 to today.

Chapter 1 focuses on the late 19th century. The discussion was largely about the transition from slavery to emancipation, and establishing basic human and civil rights for former slaves and other people of color and their descendants.

Chapter 2 centers on The Times's coverage in the early 20th century, when the goal was to make the promise of equality a reality.

The early civil rights struggles exploded in the 1950s and 1960s into protests spearheaded by galvanizing figures such as Malcolm X and Dr. Martin Luther King Jr. Chapter 3 delves into the catalysts and consequences of this incendiary time.

From the 1970s on, overt racism in the United States has, to some extent, diminished. But racism hasn't gone away. Rather, it persists in institutional practices and policies. Chapter 4 looks at race relations through stories about the disproportionate killing of people of color by

Protesters held hands in silent protest at a rally in Union Square in New York City to protest the acquittal of George Zimmerman. A neighborhood watch volunteer, Mr. Zimmerman was accused of murder, having fatally shot 17-year-old high-school student Trayvon Martin in Sandford, Fla., in 2012. Mr. Martin was black.

police officers, the trend toward resegregation in American schools, and Supreme Court rulings that will have indelible effects.

After the election of President Barack Obama in 2008, some people began talking about the United States being a "post-racial" society. The idea was that President Obama's election meant that race was a social construct the country had outgrown. Race wasn't real, and it was no longer necessary to talk about it.

Today, as social movements such as Black Lives Matter make clear, the idea of a post-racial America was premature, and likely naïve. Race is real. It matters. And it is urgent that we learn as much as possible about the ways that concepts of race are socially constructed and reinforced so that we might make a future post-racial society possible.

CHAPTER 1

From Slavery to Emancipation

The New York Times began covering race relations at its start in 1851. Early editions of the newspaper featured stories of fugitive slaves and the ideas of free black men, conflicts between settlers and American Indians, and the difference in perception between ambitious Chinese workers and the California government. Articles supported the abolition of slavery, but not those who broke the law to fight for it. The paper lauded President Abraham Lincoln's Emancipation Proclamation and the ratification of the 13th, 14th and 15th Amendments.

The Chaplin Case

BY THE NEW YORK TIMES | SEPT. 24, 1851

W. L. CHAPLIN. — We learn from the Baltimore Argus that the bail in the case of Mr. Chaplin, the abolitionist, has not only been forfeited, but the money — nineteen thousand dollars — paid into the treasury of Maryland.

Here is a curious fact in the history of fanaticism. This man, Chaplin, through some process of reasoning or other, believes it to be his duty to aid slaves in gaining their liberty; and addicts himself, therefore, to enticing them to run away. His offence is clearly theft, for they are the legal property of their masters. And to screen from punishment this high man, of diseased sympathies if not intellect, the immense sum of nineteen thousand dollars is paid into a Maryland Court. There must be sincerity at the bottom of such a sacrifice. It is the sincerity of fanaticism — of men whose whole mental and moral faculties have been subjected to a single idea. But it cannot fail to be powerful when it leads to such sacrifices. We regret that Chaplin has thus evaded the punishment he deserved; but we cannot help admiring the attachment of friends which showed itself by so strong a proof.

The Colored Race

BY THE NEW YORK TIMES | SEPT. 27, 1851

WE HAVE RECEIVED two or three sharp letters severely censuring us for alleged injustice towards the colored race. They are all based upon our remarks concerning Chaplin's case, in which we denounced his efforts to induce slaves to run away from their masters, as a violation of law, and as springing from a " diseased sympathy."

We see no reason to change our opinion or our language. We believe slavery to be an evil, quite as earnestly as any of our censors. We wish some feasible plan could be devised to get rid of it. We believe that it is deeply injurious to any society in which it exists, and that it deprives its subjects of rights — which belong to them in common with the whole human race. We hope the time will come when all parties and all classes of men in this country will be willing to look at the subject dispassionately, and to devise some means whereby the rights of the slave can be restored, and yet the rights of the master not impaired.

Mr. Chaplin may be a benevolent and a conscientious man, for ought we know. We know nothing whatever of his character or his life, except that he went to Washington and attempted to get sundry slaves away from their masters. This, in our view, was an outrage and a wrong. It was calculated to deprive the master of property recognized and protected by law, without paying for it in any way. It excited ill-feeling, where good feeling alone can produce good results. It made Southern masters jealous and suspicious of the North, and gave color to the belief that the North was willing to aid a crusade against their institutions and rights.

Any such belief will only retard the enfranchisement of the enslaved and render still more difficult all endeavors to improve his condition. We have no objection to efforts to liberate the slave, provided they are made with due regard to the interests and rights of other classes of the community. If abolitionists or others, desire to set free any one, ten or a hundred slaves, let them raise money to buy them of their masters. The effort may be more difficult, but it will be far more praise-worthy, and in the end far more successful than such clandestine endeavors to aid their escape, as that in which Mr. Chaplin was engaged.

One of the letters to which we referred, contains the following paragraph:

> Dear Sir: The first Daily Times came in my hands this morning. In perusing the matter, (especially editorial) I was much surprised at the position you have taken in opposite to the advancement of the poor, despised and ever-hated, my own people, the people of Color. In your article it is plain to infer that you, too, are an additional battlement, just erected, to strike at our very soul's existence, which are the rights of common humanity. And for what cause or for what interests, I am unable to explain. Why The Times of this morning, under the head of the Chaplin case, should so insinuatingly endeavor to degrade more, if possible, in the eyes of the country, the colored people, I cannot understand.

We assure our correspondent that he is entirely mistaken. We would not lay one straw in the way of the advancement and improvement of the colored race. Their fate is hard enough already to excite emotions of pity in any heart which can feel at all. But how is their welfare to be best promoted? By enticing those of them who are slaves away from their masters, and then throwing them, helpless and friendless as they are, upon the charities of Northern society? Is the condition of the free blacks at the North so enviable as to render it desirable to swell their number indefinitely? And even if it were, are their masters to be robbed of their property without compensation?

Our correspondent will find us friendly to every proper effort that he or any one else may make to improve the condition of the free negroes in the Northern States. We will cheerfully aid every endeavor to educate them, and to elevate their character and condition. And we will gladly cooperate in any measure to release slaves from their bondage, with the consent and compensation of their masters, and without infringing the rights or injuring the interests of any other class. But we shall not countenance robbery, even when the perpetrator of it may think he is doing right. We believe any sentiment which prompts one man to seek to deprive another of his property, even if that property be in a slave, without his consent and to his injury, to be, at the least, diseased, we will not consent to "do evil" even "that good may come."

Arrest of a Fugitive Slave

BY THE NEW YORK TIMES | DEC. 9, 1851

A COLORED MAN named W. Henry, who has resided in this city for some time past, was arrested this morning by U. S. Marshal Allen, as a fugitive slave. He is a cooper by trade, and was at work in his shop when he was arrested. The officer informed him that he was charged with some slight offence, and he allowed himself to be taken and handcuffed under that impression. He was taken before Commissioner Saline, and an examination gone into.

Considerable excitement was occasioned by the arrest, and a large crowd assembled in and about the office of the Commissioner. While the examination was progressing, the negro made his escape into the street, and was closely followed by a crowd of persons; some of whom were desirous to assist in his escape, and others were equally desirous to assist in his recapture. A carriage was speedily procured by the negro's friends, but not in season to be made available for the object in view. He was recaptured by the officers before he got out of the limits of the city. He was taken to the police office, followed by a large crowd, composed mostly of his friends. Nothing further was done with the examination up to 7 o'clock, but the military were ordered out, and all arrangements made to carry the law into effect. What will be the end no one can tell.

An Indian Encounter.

BY THE NEW YORK TIMES | SEPT. 22, 1851

SPANISH BAR, AUG. 8 — On the 4th inst., while Mr S. Jackson, of the State of New-York, and W. J. Bruce, an Irishman, were traveling from Junction Bar to Grey Eagle City, they fell in with a company of Indians, between the North and Middle Forks, on the Ridge Trail, about seven miles distant from here, who, at first, appeared kindly disposed, in return for which my friends distributed among them a few pounds of crackers. After they separated, Mr. J. and his companion had not proceeded far, when they observed an Indian crossing their trail; they at once suspected an attack, and were not mistaken, as a shower of arrows soon convinced them of their perilous situation. Although they had but one revolver and a bowie-knife, yet they determined not to fly, and taking their position behind a shelving rock close by, they awaited the appearance of their opponents, and in a few minutes twelve or fourteen of the Indians rounded the cliff behind which they were sheltered. On their first appearance, my friend, who had the revolver, discharged two barrels, one of which took effect. The assailants soon disappeared, but not before their arrows had pierced both my friends; one received a severe wound in the arm and the other in the thigh.

They pursued the Indians some distance through the brushwood till they came to an opening, where they halted to consult whether or not it would be expedient for them to continue the chase. While thus consulting, they observed Indians a short distance ahead, collected together, evidently preparing for another attack. Flight seemed the only recourse now, and they again sought refuge in the shelf of an adjoining rock, where they lay in ambush till their pursuers came up, when the one that had the revolver again fired three shots. This hot and unexpected reception terminated the chase — the entire party, save the two unfortunate recipients of the lead, one of whom yelled most fearfully, quickly disappeared. The fortunate victors, changing their route, steered for the river, and proceeded about two miles, when they met with a party of six miners, who were out prospecting for quartz veins, who dressed their wounds, and provided them a temporary home in their camp.

FROM THE MARYSVILLE HERALD

On Thursday or Friday, a couple of Indians, supposed to be from Yuba City, were caught on the other side of Yuba river; near Rose's or Brophy's ranch, stealing watermelons. They were soundly flogged and then thrown into the river. The flogging was well enough, but the throwing into the river was "too much like Indian" on the part of the white men. Whether the Indians got out of the river or were drowned, we do not know, but they have not been heard of since,

On Sunday, a party of Indians from Yuba City went in search of the missing men, but did not find them, and returned to Yuba City. On Sunday, also, the whites in the neighborhood of Rose's gathered to the number of about forty, and came down to Yuba City to "have a time." Eight or nine of them crossed Feather River to Yuba City; the rest remained on this side. The party who went over to the *rancheadero* told the Indians there that they came in search of an Indian who had been up Yuba River for the purpose of "hanging somebody." The Indians told them that if any of their number had done wrong, they would deliver him or them to the whites for punishment, if they would point out the guilty ones. This they could not do. Presently an Indian was seen crossing the river. One of the whites sang out, "there's the d—d scoundrel now!" and commenced firing upon him. The Indians knew that he was an innocent man who lived some distance up Feather River, and had just come down. They therefore commenced a fire upon the whites, and in the meantime the Indian who was crossing the river made his escape. The white men then fired once upon the Indians, and ran away. Several were wounded on either side, but no one killed,

The citizens Yuba City called a meeting and passed resolutions strongly condemnatory of the course of the whites. Appearances certainly indicate that they went, there to make a wanton attack upon the poor Indians from motives of pure maliciousness.

Letter of the Chinamen to his Excellency, Gov. Bigler.

LETTER | BY THE NEW YORK TIMES | JUNE 5, 1852

SAN FRANCISCO, THURSDAY, APRIL 29, 1852 — Sir: The Chinamen have learned with sorrow that you have published a message against them. Although we are Asiatics, some of us have been educated in American schools and have learned your language which has enabled us to read your message in the newspapers for ourselves, and to explain it to the rest of our countrymen. We have all thought a great deal about it and after consultation with one another, we have determined to write you as decent and respectful a letter as we could, pointing out to your Excellency some of the errors you have fallen into about us.

When you speak of laws of your own country, we shall not presume to contradict you. In ours, all great men are learned men, and a man's rank is just according to his education. Keying, who made the treaty with Mr. Cushing, was not only a cousin of the Emperor, but one of the most learned men in the Empire, otherwise he would not have been Governor of Canton. Just so, we doubt not, it is in California and other enlightened countries. But it will not be making little of your attainments to suppose that you do not know as much about our people as you do your own.

You speak of the Chinamen as "Coolies," and in one sense the word is applicable to a great many of them; but not in that in which you seem to use it. "Cooly" is not a Chinese word: it has been imported into China from foreign parts, as it has been into this country. What its original signification was, we do not know; but with us it means a common laborer, and nothing more. We have never known it used among us as a designation of a class, such as you have in view — persons bound to labor under contracts which they can be forcibly compelled to comply with. The Irishmen who are engaged in digging down your hills, the men who unload ships, who clean your streets, or even drive your drays, would, if they were in China, be considered "Coolies;" tradesmen, mechanics of every kind, and professional men would not. If you mean by "Coolies," laborers, many of our countrymen in the mines are "Coolies," and many again are not. There are among them tradesmen, mechanics, gentry, (being persons of respectability and who enjoy a certain rank and privilege,) and schoolmasters, who are reckoned with the gentry, and with us considered a respectable class of people. None are "Coolies," if by that word you mean bound men or contract slaves.

The ship *Challenge*, of which you speak in your message as bringing over more than five hundred Chinamen did not bring over one who was under "Cooly" contract labor. Hab-Wa, who came in here as agent for the charterers, one of the signers of this letter, states to your Excellency that they were all passengers, and are going to work in the mines for themselves.

As to our countrymen coming over here to labor for $3 or $4 per month wages, it is unreasonable on the face of it, and it is not true. That strong affection which they have for their own country, which induces them to return with the gold they dig, as you say, would prevent them from leaving their homes for wages so little, if at all better than they could get there. The Chinamen are indeed remarkable for their love of their country in a domestic way. They gather together in clans, in districts and neighborhoods, and in some villages there are thousands and thousands of the same surname, flocking around the original family home. They honor their parents and age generally with a respect like religion, and have the deepest anxiety to provide for their descendants. To honor his parents is the great duty of the son. A Chinese proverb runs somewhat in this way: "In the morning, when you rise, inquire after your parents' health, at midday be not far from them, and in the evening comfort them when they go to rest; this it is to be a pious son." With such feelings as these, it is to be expected that they will return with their gains to their homes, but it is foolish to believe they will leave them for trifling inducements.

To the same cause you must look for the reason why there are no Chinese drunkards in your streets, nor convicts in your prisons, madmen in your hospitals, or others who are a charge to your State. They live orderly, work hard, and take care of themselves, that they may have the means of providing for their homes and living amidst their families. The other matter which you allude to, their leaving their families in pledge as security for the performance of their contract, is still more inconsistent with their character, and absurd. Have you ever inquired what the holder of such a pledge could do with them? If he used any force towards them, he would be guilty of an offence, and be punished by the laws, just as in any other country, and if he treated them well, they would only be a burden and an additional expense to him. Sometimes very rich persons who have poor men in their employment at home or abroad support their families through charity, particularly if they are relatives. Sometimes they bind themselves to do it by their contracts, but this gives them no power over them as hostages or pledges.

We will tell you how it is that the Chinese poor come to California. Some have borrowed the small amount necessary, to be returned with unusual interest, on account of the risk; some have been furnished with money without interest by their friends and relations, and some again, but much the smaller portion, have received advances in money, to be returned out of the profits of the adventure. The usual apportionment of the profits is about three-tenths to the lender of the money, and rarely if ever any more. These arrangements made at home seldom bring them further than San Francisco, and here the Chinese traders furnish them the means of getting to the mines A great deal of money is thus lent at a nominal or very low interest, which, to the credit of our countrymen, we are able to say is almost invariably faithfully repaid. The poor Chinaman does not come here as a slave. He comes because of his desire for independence, and he is assisted by the charity of his countrymen which they bestow on him safely, because he is industrious and honestly repays them. When he gets to the mines he sets to work with patience, industry, temperance and economy. He gives no man any offence, and he is contented with small gains, perhaps only two or three dollars per day. His living costs him something, and he is well pleased if he saves up three or four hundred dollars a year. Like all other nations, and as is particularly to be expected of them, many return home with their money, there to remain, buy rice fields, build houses and devote themselves to the society of their own households and the increase of the products of their country, of its exports and imports, of its commerce and the general wealth of the world. But not all; others — full as many as of other nations — invest their gains in merchandise and bring it into the country and sell it at your markets. It is possible, sir, that you may not be aware how great this trade is, and how rapidly it is increasing, and how many are now returning to California as merchants who came over originally as miners. We are not able to tell you how much has been paid by Chinese importers at the Custom House, but the sum must be very large. In this city alone there are twenty stores kept by Chinamen, who own the lots and erected the buildings themselves. In these stores a great deal of business is done; all kinds of Chinese goods — rice, silks, sugar, tea, &c. — are sold in them, and also a great quantity of American goods, especially boots, of which every Chinaman buys one or more pairs immediately on landing. And then there are the American stores dealing in Chinese articles on a very large scale, and some with the most remarkable success. The emigration of the "Coolies," as your Excellency rather mistakingly calls us, is attended with the opening of all this Chinese trade, which if it produces the same results here as elsewhere, will yet be the pride and riches of this city and State. One of the subscribers of this letter is now employed as a clerk in an American store, because of the services he can render them as a broker in business with his countrymen; he has sometimes sold $10,000 a day of Chinese goods. Chy Lung, who arrived a few days since with some $10,000 in China goods, has sold out and returns for another cargo, on the *Challenge*. Fei-Chaong, who brought in a cargo about month ago, has sold out, and also returns in the *Challenge*. So does the partner of Sam Wa of this city;

Tuk-Shaong for the same purpose — for more than a year he has been continually importing and selling cargoes. A great many others send for goods by the *Challenge*, and all the other ships which you speak of as being expected, will bring cargoes of Chinese goods as well as Chinamen. Nor does this by any means give you a full idea of the trade of the Chinamen. They not only freight your ships, but they have bought many of them, and will buy more; and as to the freighting of ships it may be worthy of your attention to know, that such is our preference for your countrymen, that we employ your ships in preference to any others, even when we could get them cheaper. When a ship arrives, every body sees how actively and profitably your drays, steamboats, wagons, etc., are employed by us. Some of us read in the papers the other day that the Government of the United States were going to send ships to Japan, to open that country to American trade. That is what we supposed your country wished with China as well as other countries, but it cannot all be on one side, and it is plain that the more advantages we get from your country, the faster you will get the benefits of our trade. The gold we have been allowed to dig in your mines is what has made the China trade grow up so fast, like every thing else in this country. If you want to check immigration from Asia, you will have to do it by checking Asiatic commerce, which we supposed from all that we have ever known of your Government, the United States most desired to increase.

What your Excellency has said about passing a law to prevent Coolies shipped to California under contracts from laboring in the mines, we do not conceive concerns us, for there are none such here from China, nor do we believe any are coming, except a small number, perhaps who work on shares, as we have before explained, just as people from all other countries sometimes do. We will not believe it is your intention to pass a law treating us as Coolies whether we are so or not. You say there is no treaty provision for the manner in which Chinese emigrants shall be treated, and that the Chinese government would have no right to complain of any law excluding us from the country, by taxation or otherwise. This may be true of the Government, but it would certainly alienate the present remarkably friendly feelings of the Chinese people, and in many ways interfere with the full enjoyments of the commercial privileges guaranteed to the Americans by the treaty of Wang-Hiya.

In what we here say we have most carefully told your Excellency the truth, but we fear you will not believe us, because you have spoken in your message of us as Asiatics, "ignorant of the solemn character of the oath or affirmation in the form prescribed in the Constitution and statutes," or "indifferent to the solemn obligation to speak the truth which an oath imposes." It is truth, nevertheless, and we leave it to time and the proof which our words carry in them to satisfy you of the fact. It has grieved us that you should publish so bad a character of us, and we wish that you could change your opinion and speak well of us to the public. We do not deny that many Chinamen tell lies, and so do many Americans, even in Courts of Justice. But we have our Courts, too, and our forms of oaths, which are as sacredly respected by our countrymen as other nations respect theirs. We do not swear upon so many little occasions as you do, and our forms will seem as ridiculous to you as yours do to us when we first see them. You will smile when we tell you that on ordinary occasions an oath is attested by burning a piece of yellow paper, and on the more important ones by cutting off the head of a cock; yet these are only forms, and cannot be of great importance, we would think. But in the important matters we are good men; we honor our parents; we take care of our children; we are industrious and peaceable; we trade much; we are trusted for small and large sums; we pay our debts and are honest; and of course must tell the truth. Good men cannot tell lies and be ignorant of the difference between right and. wrong. We do not think much about your politics, but we believe you are mistaken in supposing no Chinaman has ever yet applied to be naturalized or has acquired a domicil in the United States except here. There is a Chinaman now in San Francisco who is said to be a naturalized citizen, and to have a free white

American wife. He wears the American dress, and is considered a man of respectability. And there are, or were lately, we are informed, Chinamen residing in Boston, New-York, and New-Orleans. If the privileges of your laws are open to us, some of us will doubtless acquire your habits, your language, your ideas, your feelings, your morals, your forms, and become citizens of your country — many have already adopted your religion as their own — and we will be good citizens. There are very good Chinamen now in the country, and a better class will, if allowed, come hereafter — men of learning and of wealth, bringing their families with them.

In concluding this letter, we will only beg your Excellency not to be too hasty with us, to find us out and know us well, and then we are certain you will not command your Legislature to make laws driving us out of your country. Let us stay here — the Americans are doing good to us, and we will do good to them.

Your most humble servants,
Hab Wa, Sam Wo & Co.
Long Achick, Ton Wo & Co.
For the Chinamen in California.

Douglas vs. Douglass, Settlement of Nebraska

BY THE NEW YORK TIMES | OCT. 13, 1854

ARNOLD DOUGLAS having forced upon the country his plan for getting Slavery into Kansas, Mr. Frederick Douglass announces his plan for keeping Slavery out of it. This plan is simply the settlement in Kansas, at the earliest possible period, of a large and well disciplined body of free Colored people from the Northern States. "There is nothing," says Mr. Douglass, "confessedly, which the slaveholder more dreads than the presence of a numerous population of industrious, enlightened, and orderly Colored men. Where they are to be, he will be careful not to come."

Mr. Douglass having carefully examined all the information possible to be obtained from those who have traversed the Territory or resided in it, declares, in a manifesto recently issued by him, that their testimony uniformly and conclusively leads to the conclusion that the climate, soil and productions are *precisely such as are best adapted to develop the energies of Colored laborers, reared in the Middle and Northern States of the Union.* It is not to be denied that, whether reasonable or not, there is in the minds of our most intelligent and wealthy colored people, an insurmountable objection to emigration to Liberia, and Mr. Douglass is satisfied that it is in every way better for them to emigrate to Kansas than to the West Indies or Central America, to which lately many of them have been inclined. Mr. Douglass estimates that there are in the City of New-York and its vicinity, three hundred families of African blood, who, if proper means "be taken, can be induced to emigrate to Kansas. In Philadelphia and Cincinnati, six hundred additional families will be obtained. Boston and New-England will furnish at least one hundred, making altogether an army of one thousand families as an immediate colonial nucleus. One hundred of these families will form a town in some central position favorable to commerce and manufactures; the remaining nine hundred will be

The abolitionist Frederick Douglass in 1848.

spread in a circle of twenty-five or fifty miles of this emporium. It is then hoped and believed that all will go manfully and soberly to work, minding their own business, respecting the just rights of each other and of other settlers in the Territory with whom they may come in contact, and thus Kansas may be secured to freedom without conflict, without bloodshed, and without Government interference. That those interested in extending the power of Slavery would threaten to interfere to prevent the execution of the plan, is to be presumed. They have already threatened and resolved that the emigration of Freedom-loving white men to the Territory should be prevented by lawless force. They have talked bravely of bowie-knives and revolvers, but the only effect of all this has probably been to increase emigration from the Free States, and Mr. Douglass, speaking for the colored men of the North, considers it worthy only of his good-natured derision.

Mr. Douglass asks that an Association be at once formed to promote the emigration of free colored people to Kansas. Branch Associations should be organized in each of the large cities mentioned, and in any other communities where there are considerable numbers of colored people, who should employ agents — men capable of inspiring confidence — to bring the subject properly before them and aid such as are disposed to go with funds if necessary, but especially by helping them to associate efficiently, and by procuring them the best advice and information. It is believed that $40,000, systematically and skillfully used, would establish in Kansas the whole colony of one thousand families. Those who pity or blame the disposition of colored people to congregate together in cities are especially called upon to move in this scheme, and the assistance of the press is solicited to bring the subject properly before the public.

Why Mr. Douglass thinks it advisable to form especial Associations for this purpose, unless he has seen reason to doubt the earnestness and efficiency of the existing Emigrants Aid Societies, we do not know.

The policy of these Societies seems to have been thus far directed to sending to Kansas a few reliable and trustworthy men as the initiatory agents of emigration, to obtain information and prepare the way, as a discreet advanced-guard for the great stream of emigration which they have promised to pour in this Fall. We presume they are now nearly prepared to commence their main undertaking, and that in a few weeks our streets and roadsides will be profusely posted with announcements of the cheap facilities which they have secured for the transportation of all persons who are willing to settle Kansas in the interest of Freedom.

The first of the new Boston line of Kansas Emigrant packets, under the energetic direction of the noble merchant princes of New-England, may already have been quietly dispatched to Rotterdam, and will be the first transport of the "Army of Freemen" which agents of the Society have been recruiting during the Summer in the Rhenish provinces of Prussia. Probably in another month, when the frosts shall have removed all danger to strangers in the valleys of the Mississippi and Missouri, at least one-third of the ten thousand emigrants now arriving weekly at our ports from Europe, will be directed to Kansas, with the benefit of the extraordinary facilities of transportation thither, and of settlement in comfort when there, which the advantages of association and cooperation of capital and capitalists shall have secured for them.

Such names as Lawrence and Grinnell are never associated with sleepy and ill-directed enterprises, and we see no reason why the Free Colored Emigration should be made a specialty, unless it is that, for its own success, and their honor, it might better be organized and directed in the first place by intelligent colored citizens themselves. That there are men of sufficient ability among them for this purpose, if they were properly encouraged and sustained by the public at large, there can be no doubt.

The laws of the country, we hardly need say, oppose no objections to this project. With all the injustice and meanness which was crowded into the Nebraska bill, its author forgot to make provision to exclude colored citizens from the territory, and although the Homestead bill denies them the legal right of preemption claimants, such is the character of the population which it is now to be hoped will occupy Kansas, that Mr. Douglass fears not to trust to their honor, magnanimity and common sense to be superior to law. This he may certainly do with safety as far as regards that class of population which has thus far gone from this quarter, and equally so with that which is expected to arrive from Germany, with which it is well known there is no such prejudice against the colored people as so generally obtains among the lower classes of the Anglo-Saxon race. But the plan proposed, of settling the colored people in a strong community by themselves, removes any danger which might be supposed to exist, of their being robbed of hard-earned improvements by Southerners or by any one who is not inclined to neighborly association with them. That the colony, once founded, will be rapidly recruited even from the Slave States themselves, is extremely probable. We know that in Louisiana especially, there are many colored men of wealth and education, who would be glad to emigrate on account of the deterioration of the land which they at present occupy, or for other reasons, who will not come North on account of their dread of the cold climate, and who are prevented from going westward by the laws of Texas, which authorize the apprehension and sale into Slavery of any colored man found in the State, who is not claimed within a year as the existing property of a white man.

That such a colony in Kansas will have the effect which Mr. Douglass anticipates, no one will doubt who knows the dread which planters everywhere have of their slaves witnessing the prosperity of free negroes. "Let it be known throughout the country that one thousand colored families, provided with all the needful implements of pioneers, and backed up by the moral influence of the Northern people, are to take up their abode in Kansas, and slaveholders, who are now bent upon blasting that fair land with Slavery, would shun it as if it were infested by famine, pestilence and earthquakes." There could be no better guard against Negro Slavery than such a garrison of Negro Freemen. If it be said that there are already all-sufficient means in operation to keep Slavery out of Kansas, the answer is, Slavery is already there, and there is reason to believe that while many good and true men are going to that territory who can neither be frightened nor bought into supporting Slavery, there are others, especially from the population of Slave State origin of Indiana and Illinois, who are of quite a different stamp, and who, in connection with those who come direct from the Slave States, may be sufficient in numbers to control the first elections, the time for which will soon arrive, unless, indeed, the immigration of free-minded foreigners should be made greater than has yet been indicated.

Southern slaveholders in a conflict like this are hard to beat, as experience has long taught us; and certainly it is unwise, as Mr. Douglass urges, where there is so much at stake, and when the right is so clearly on our side, to omit any effort or neglect any plan to secure a victory for Freedom — a victory which may be decisive of the whole controversy of Slavery in the Republic forever.

Decision of the Supreme Court in the Dred Scott Case — The Position of Slavery in the Constitution.

BY THE NEW YORK TIMES | MARCH 9, 1857

THE OPINION OF THE Supreme Court in the Dred Scott case was delivered by Chief Justice Tahey. It won a full and elaborate statement of the views of the Court. They have decided the following important points:

First — Negroes, whether slaved or free, that is, men of the African race, are not citizens of the United States by the Constitution.

Second — The Ordinance of 1787 had no independent constitutional force or legal offset subsequently to the adoption of the Constitution, and could not operate of itself to confer freedom or citizenship within the Northwest Territory on negroes not citizens by the Constitution.

Third — The provisions of the Act of 1820 commonly called the Missouri Compromise, in so far as it undertook to exclude negro slavery from and communicate freedom and citizenship to, negroes in the northern part of the Louisiana caisson, was a Legislative act exceeding the powers of Congress, and void, and of no legal effect to that end.

In deciding those main points, the Supreme Court determined the following incidental points:

First — The expression "territory and other property" of the Union, in the Constitution, applies "in terms" only to such territory as the Union possessed at the time of the adoption of the Constitution,

Second — The rights of citizens of the United States emigrating into any Federal territory, and the power of the Federal Government there depend on the general provisions of the Constitution, which defines in this, as in all other respects, the powers of Congress.

Third — As Congress does not possess power itself to make enactments relative to the persons or property or citizens of the United States, in a Federal Territory, other than such as the Constitution confers, so it cannot constitutionally delegate any such powers to a Territorial Government, organised by it under the Constitution.

Fourth — The legal condition of a slave in the State of Missouri is not affected by the temporary sojourn of such slave in any other State, but on his return his condition still depends on the laws of Missouri.

As the plaintiff was not a citizen of Missouri, he, therefore, could not sue in the Courts of the United States. The suit must be dismissed for want of jurisdiction.

The delivery of this opinion occupied about three hours, and was listened to with profound attention by a crowded courtroom. Among the auditors were gentlemen of eminent legal ability, and a due proportion of ladies.

Judge Nelson stated the merits of the case. The question was whether or not the removal of Scott from Missouri with his master to Illinois, with a view to temporary residence there, worked his emancipation He maintained that the question depended wholly on the law of Missouri, and for that reason the judgment of the Court below should be affirmed.

Judge Catron believed the Supreme Court has jurisdiction to decide the merits of the case. He argued that Congress could not do directly what it could not do indirectly. If it could exclude one species of property, it could exclude another. With regard to the Territories coded, Congress could govern them only with the restrictions of the States which ceded them; and the Missouri act of 1820 violated the leading features of the Constitution, and was therefore void. He concurred with his brother judges that Scott is a slave, and was so when this suit was brought.

Several other Judges are to deliver their views tomorrow.

Emancipation. President Lincoln's Proclamation.

THE NEW YORK TIMES | JAN. 3, 1863

WASHINGTON, THURSDAY, JAN. 1, 1863 — *By the President of the United States of America — a Proclamation:*

Whereas, on the twenty-second day of September, in the year of our Lord one thousand eight hundred and sixty-two, a Proclamation was issued by the President of the United States containing among other things the following, to wit:

That on the first day of January, in the year of our Lord, one thousand eight hundred and sixty-three, all persons held as slaves within any State or designated part of a State, the people whereof shall there be in rebellion against the United States, shall be then, thenceforth, and *forever free*; and the Executive Government of the United States, including the Military and Naval authority thereof will recognize and maintain the freedom of such persons, and will do no act or acts to repress such persons or any of them in any effort they may make for their actual freedom. That the Executive will, on the first day of January aforesaid, by Proclamation, designate the States and parts of States, if any, in which the people therein, respectively, shall then be in rebellion against the United States, and the fact that any State or the people thereof, shall on that day be in good faith be presented in the Congress of the United States by Members chosen thereto at elections wherein a majority of the qualified voters of such States shall have participated, shall in the absence of strong countervailing testimony, be deemed conclusive evidence that such State and the people thereof, are not then in rebellion against the United States.

Now, therefore, I, Abraham Lincoln, President of the United States, by virtue of the power in me vested, as Commander-in-Chief of the Army and Navy of the United States, in time of actual armed rebellion against the authority and Government of the United States, and as a fit and necessary war measure for suppressing said rebellion, do, on this first day of January, in the year of our Lord one thousand eight hundred and sixty-three, and in accordance with my purpose so to do publicly proclaimed for the full period of one hundred days from the day of the first above-mentioned, order and designate as the States and parts of States wherein the people thereof respectively are this day in rebellion against the United States, the following, to wit:

Arkansas, Texas, Louisiana — except the Parishes of St. Bernard, Picquemines, Jefferson, St. John, St. Charles , St. James Ascension, Assumption, Terrebonne, Lafourche, St. Mary, St. Martin, and Orleans, including the City of New-Orleans — Mississippi, Alabama, Florida, Georgia, South Carolina, North Carolina, and Virginia — except the forty-eight counties designated as West Virginia, and also the counties of Berkley, Accomac, Northampton, Elizabeth City, York, Princess Ann and Norfolk, including the cities of Norfolk and Portsmouth, and which excepted parts, are for the present, left precisely as if this proclamation were not issued.

And, by virtue of the power, and for the purpose aforesaid, I do aver and declare that all persons held as slaves within said designated States and parts of States are and henceforward, shall be free, and that the Executive Government of the United States, including the military and naval authorities thereof will recognize and maintain the freedom of said persons.

And I hereby enjoin upon the people so declared to be free, to abstain from all violence unless in necessary self-defence, and I recommend to them that in all cases, when allowed, they labor faithfully for reasonable wages.

And I further declare and make known that such persons of suitable condition, will be received into the armed service of the United States, to garrison forts, positions, stations, and other places, and to man vessels of all sorts in said service.

And, upon this — sincerely believed to be an act of justice, warranted by the Constitution — upon military necessity — I invoke the considerate judgment of mankind and the gracious favor of Almighty God.

In witness whereof I have hereunto set my hand and caused the seal of the United States to be affixed.

Done at the City of Washington, this first day of January, in the year of Our Lord one thousand eight hundred and sixty-three, and of the independence of the United States of America the eighty-seven.

By the President: ABRAHAM LINCOLN.

WM. H. SEWARD, Secretary of State.

The President's Proclamation

BY THE NEW YORK TIMES | JAN. 3, 1863

PRESIDENT LINCOLN'S PROCLAMATION, which we publish this morning, marks an era in the history, not only of this war, but of this country and the world. It is not necessary to assume that it will set free instantly the enslaved blacks of the South, in order to ascribe to it the greatest and most permanent importance. Whatever may be its immediate results, it changes entirely the relations of the National Government to the institution of Slavery. Hitherto Slavery has been under the protection of the Government; henceforth it is under its ban. The power of the Army and Navy, hitherto employed in hunting and returning to bondage the fugitive from service, are to be employed in maintaining his freedom whenever and wherever he may choose to assert it. This change of attitude is itself a revolution.

President Lincoln takes care, by great precision in his language, to define the basis on which this action rests. He issues the Proclamation "as a fit and necessary war measure for suppressing the rebellion." While he sincerely believes it to be an "act of justice warranted by the Constitution." he issues it "upon military necessity." In our judgment it is only upon that ground and for that purpose that he has any right to issue it at all. In his civil capacity as President, he has not the faintest shadow of authority to decree the emancipation of a single slave, either as an "act of justice" or for any other purpose whatever. As Commander-in-Chief of the army he has undoubtedly the right to deprive the rebels of the aid of their slaves — just as he has the right to take their horses, and to arrest all persons who may be giving them aid and comfort "as a war measure" and upon grounds of military necessity.

It may seem at first sight a matter of small importance in what capacity the act is done.

But its validity may, in the end, depend upon that very point. Sooner or later his action in this matter will come up for review before the

Supreme Court and it is a matter of the utmost importance to the President, to the slaves, and to the country, that it should come in a form to be sustained. It must be a legal and a constitutional act, in form as well as in substance. We wish that for this reason the President had given it the form of a Military Order — addressed to his subordinate Generals, enjoining upon them specific acts in the performance of their military duties — instead of a Proclamation addressed to the world at large, and embodying declarations and averments instead of commands.

What effect the Proclamation will have remains to be seen. We do not think that it will at once set free any considerable number of slaves beyond the actual and effective jurisdiction of our armies. It will lead to no immediate insurrections, and involve no massacres, except such as the rebels in the blindness of their wrath may themselves set on foot. The slaves have no arms, are without organization, and in dread of the armed and watchful whites. Besides, they evince no disposition to fight for themselves so long as they see that we are fighting for them. They understand, beyond all question, that the tendency of this war is to give them freedom, and that the Union armies, whatever may be their motive, are actually and practically fighting for their liberty. If the war should suddenly end, if they should see the fighting stop, and the Constitution which protects Slavery restored to full vigor in the Slave States, their disappointment would vent itself in the wrathful explosion of insurrection and violence. But so long as the war continues, we look for nothing of that kind. Whenever our armies reach their immediate vicinity, they will doubtless assert their freedom, and call upon us to "recognize and maintain" it. Until then, they will work for their masters and wait for deliverance.

President Lincoln "recommends" the enfranchised slaves, "in all cases, when allowed, to labor faithfully for reasonable wages." That great question, before the end is reached, will demand other treatment than this. If the President supposes that millions of men, who never made a bargain in their lives, who were never consulted on any subject affecting their own interest, who never made provision for their own support, or had the slightest charge connected with the maintenance of wives or children, and who have worked all their lives under the pressure of force and fear, can pass suddenly to the condition of free men — recognizing at once all its responsibilities and performing all its duties — he must believe that the age of miracles is not yet past. If the Proclamation makes the slaves actually free, there will come the further duty of making them work.

That the whole negro race is to remain idle if it should choose so to do, being free, no one can seriously propose. If the slaves choose to "labor faithfully for reasonable wages" — very well — they will establish their claim to freedom by the highest of titles, the ability to use and enjoy it. But if they do not, they must be compelled to do it — not by brute force, nor by being owned like cattle, and denied every human right, but by just and equal laws — such laws as in every community control and forbid vagrancy, mendicancy, and all the shapes by which idle vagabondage preys upon industry and thrift.

But all this opens a vast and most difficult subject, with which we do not propose now to deal. In time, however, it will challenge universal attention, and demand for the solution of the problems which it involves the ablest and most patient statesmanship of the land.

The Consummation! Slavery Forever Dead in the United States.

BY THE NEW YORK TIMES | DEC. 19, 1865

The Thirteenth Amendment to the United States Constitution abolished slavery. It was passed by Congress on January 31, 1865, and ratified by the states on December 6, 1865.

WILLIAM H. SEWARD, Secretary of State of the United States,

To All to Whom these presents May Come, Greeting.

Know ye, that, whereas, the Congress of the United States, on the 1st of February last, passed a resolution, which is in the words following, namely:

"A resolution submitting to the Legislatures of the several States a proposition to amend the Constitution of the United States:

Resolved, By the Senate and House of Representatives of the United States of America, in Congress assembled, two-thirds of both Houses concurring, that the following article be proposed to the Legislatures of the several States as an amendment to the Constitution of the United States, which, when ratified by three-fourths of said Legislatures, shall be valid to all intents and purposes as a part of said Constitution, namely:

Article XIII.

SECTION I. *Neither slavery nor involuntary servitude, except as a punishment for crime whereof the party shall have been duly convicted, shall exist within the United States or any place subject to their jurisdiction.*

SEC. 2. *Congress shall have power to enforce this article by appropriate legislation.*

And, whereas, it appears from official documents on file in this department that the Amendment to the Constitution of the United

States proposed as aforesaid, has been ratified by the Legislatures of the States of Illinois, Rhode Island, Michigan, Maryland, New-York, West Virginia, Maine, Kansas, Massachusetts, Pennsylvania, Virginia, Ohio, Missouri, Nevada, Indiana, Louisiana, Minnesota, Wisconsin, Vermont, Tennessee, Arkansas, Connecticut, New-Hampshire, South Carolina, Alabama, North Carolina and Georgia, in all twenty-seven States;

And whereas, the whole number of States in the United States is thirty-six;

And whereas, the before specially named States, whose Legislatures have ratified the said proposed amendment, constitute three-fourths of the whole number of States in the United States;

Now, therefore, be it known that I, William H. Seward, Secretary of State of the United States, by virtue and in pursuance of the second section of the act of Congress approved the 20th of April, 1818, entitled "An Act to provide for the publication of the laws of the United States and for other purposes," do hereby certify that the amendment aforesaid *has become valid to all intents and purposes as a part of the Constitution of the United States.*

In testimony whereof, I have hereunto set my hand and caused the seal of the Department of State to be affixed. Done at the City of Washington, this 18th day of December, in the year of our Lord 1865, and of the Independence of the United States of America the 90th.

WM. H. SEWARD, Secretary of State.

The South and the Negro Vote.

FROM THE CHARLESTON MERCURY | MARCH 30, 1868

THE STATES SOUTH of Mason and Dixon's line are neither more out, nor more in the so-called Union than they were on the day before, or the day after the surrender of Gen. Lee. We are denied admission; and the denial will be accepted. The only two States who have yet voted on the question of Radical reconstruction have promptly and decisively declined to accept it upon those terms. The end is no nearer — the Union is still dissolved. The Government at Washington, actuated by passion and prejudice, and reckless lust of power, holds the States still at arm's length from each other, and still feeds the feeling of mutual distrust, and adds bitterness to bitterness.

It is just as well, men of the North, that you should understand now, as at any other time, the people of the Southern States do not intend to be ruled by negroes. It is the purpose of the United States Government to negroize the South States, they may as well know now that as any other time, that it has to be done with bayonet and has to be preserved with the bayonet in all time to come. This Southern people do not intend to be mongrelized. They prefer the sword — this they can always compel.

The policy of the Radical destructives renders perpetual a standing army in the ten Southern States. The nineteenth century, with all its bloody follies, will have sunk into the grave of the past, and Radical reconstruction will not yet have been accomplished. What crimes, what upheavals of society and Governments, what destruction of national and individual property it will effect it is impossible now distinctly to see. But that this policy, if pursued, will in one shape or another evolve these calamities there is little room for doubt.

Earnestly solicitous as the Southern people are in good faith to abide the result of unfavorable war, and to meet fairly the issue of defeat, in yielding an honest acquiescence to the premises upon which the war was declared to be fought by the United States Government — "the preservation of the Union," — this people will not debase themselves under negro rule; they will not assume the level of the negro.

The Conduct and Attitude
of the Southern Opposition

BY THE NEW YORK TIMES | SEPT. 11, 1868

Also called "black codes," slave codes were laws passed by Southern states after the Civil War to restrict the freedom of black people to be employed and paid a fair wage, to move, to own land and to testify in court. These laws were outlawed by the Fourteenth Amendment, which was ratified on July 28, 1868.

A GEORGIA CORRESPONDENT, whose letter we print elsewhere, challenges our position in regard to the South in general, and the recent expulsion from the Legislature in particular; and moreover defends that proceeding as in itself proper, and in harmony with the fixed purpose of the Southern people.

The merit of the Georgia controversy turns upon the question which our correspondent treats as settled. He assumes that in declaring colored members ineligible, the majority of the House simply asserted an incontrovertible right. That, however, is just the point to be settled. Our opinion is that, in so exercising its power, the House exceeded its authority; that, under the pretence of judging of the qualifications of its members, it violated the Constitution of the State and the Federal Constitution, both of which now ignore color as a distinctive element in the affirmation of the rights of citizens. If this view is correct, what our correspondent applauds as the exercise of a right, really was an outrage of the most flagrant character.

The Slave Code of Georgia did not designate colored persons as ineligible to office. It ignored them as a class having no lawful status as citizens. Not being citizens in the eye of the law, they had none of the rights of citizens, and in that capacity the Code took no notice of them. All this is changed by the Fourteenth Amendment, by virtue of which the National Constitution now regards all persons born or naturalized in the United States as citizens thereof, and of the State wherein they reside. By this amendment the legal effect of the Dred Scott decision is obliterated, and the black native of Georgia occupies a status as citizen as good as that of the white planter. The Slave Code ceases to be operative, so far as it imposes constitutional ineligibility on the black race; and the general reenacting clause of the new State Constitution cannot give renewed vitality to a principle which Federal authority has extinguished. Besides, the new State Constitution is decisive in the same way. It takes no note of color. It says at the outset, "all persons born or naturalized in the United States, and residents of this State, are hereby declared citizens of this State;" and it further provides, almost in the identical language of the Fourteenth Amendment, that "no law shall be made or enforced which shall abridge the privileges or immunities of citizens of the United States, or of this State." We can conceive of nothing more conclusive. It is as clear as reasoning on general principles can render anything that the plea on which the Georgia Democrats rely is worthless, and that both Federal and local organic law affirms the eligibility of the members whom they have expelled as ineligible.

We are told in reply that the Fourteenth Amendment could not be intended to embrace office-holding in its idea of the privileges or immunities to which citizens are entitled, because it distinctly contemplates the possibility of a limitation of the suffrage. Those who may be disfranchised may be made ineligible to office. The truth of this does not help the Georgia Legislature. For only by disfranchisement can ineligibility to office be wrought out; and that is a measure which entails a certain penalty on the State, and which only another Constitutional Convention can enact. The present Legislature has no authority in the premises. It has no more right to exclude from office because of color than to deprive of the suffrage for the same reason. Under the Constitution, the right to vote and the right to hold office are coextensive, and the Legislature cannot properly interfere with either. The Constitution defines the method of effecting change, and to this supreme authority the Legislature is subject.

How the wrong may be remedied is a question we are not disposed to answer with the same degree of confidence. It is a difficult and delicate question. The House has a right to decide upon the election and qualification of its members, and no State Court has jurisdiction over it. An adverse judgment may be pronounced, but the prominent advocates of expulsion have announced their intention to disregard it. They claim to be judges of law as well as of fact, and will heed no opinion or decision at variance with their action. What, then, can Congress do? May not the Senate and House in turn assert their supreme control over elections and qualifications, and respectively refuse to admit the Senators and Representatives whom Georgia will send to the next session? The inquiry is not extravagant in view of the fact that Georgia regained its privilege of self-government, in part, by ratifying the Fourteenth Amendment, which without that vote would still be law. The act of ratification, however, in the Georgia House, was carried by the votes of the colored members who have been expelled as ineligible. If they had no lawful title to seats they could have none to votes; and after striking them off, the motion to ratify becomes a failure. Interpreting the action of the Legislature in respect of the amendment in the light of its recent proceeding, no special pleading would seem necessary to justify revision by Congress on the ground of fraud. For if what purported to be a ratification was really not such, admission obtained in reliance upon it was in fact admission by false pretences; and Congress may vindicate its integrity and punish the fraud by refusing to receive the Georgia Senators and Representatives. That step would virtually be a declaration that the reconstruction of the State is still incomplete.

We have reasoned thus far on the constitutional and equitable aspects of the question, which form the bases of right. The fitness of the colored people for office, or as a race for votes, is a part of the question not at present requiring consideration. Certainly a general allegation of unfitness affords no extenuation of a proscriptive policy which ignores the ordinary tests of individual fitness. What justice demands is impartiality, whether in reference to the suffrage or office. And the Southern Democrats put themselves wholly in the wrong by discarding a just principle and installing in its place a universal prejudice against color, originating in circumstances which have ceased to exist.

That the exclusion on account of color is not to be limited to the Legislature, a subsequent resolution introduced into the Georgia House sufficiently proves. All offices are to be closed as against colored men. The letter we print exemplifies the feeling. The horror which rises before the vision of the writer is that of a time when black men shall sit beside whites in "legislative halls, in the jury box, in aldermanic duties and otherwise." The freedmen, it is evident, are to be kept down if possible, as in the days of slavery. Their civil and political bondage is to be perpetuated. Their race is to be proscribed. They are to be disfranchised and reduced to a condition of helpless dependence on their former masters. The folly of this spirit is only equaled by its cruelty and injustice. It is folly because it conflicts with established facts, which no declamation about negro inferiority can overturn. If the question now were whether the freedmen should be universally enfranchised or not, all this talk about "natural social barriers" and "the normal condition of the African" might be in order. But that stage is passed. Be it for evil or for good, colored suffrage is a fact. The freedmen have votes, of which it is no longer possible to deprive them except through the instrumentality of the new Governments. And an enfranchised power will not submit to be ruled universally out of office.

The weak point in the Georgia outrage is its conflict with local and national law. The weak point in the general position of the Southern whites who oppose reconstruction is their refusal to recognize facts which can be reversed or reformed only through specified agencies. Instead of accepting things as they are, and employing their superior intelligence and opportunities to shape and control affairs, peacefully and lawfully, they array themselves against the law and against the whole mass of colored voters, and avow a purpose to upset the local Governments and reestablish exclusive white rule by force. By taking this ground, they forfeit all title to Northern sympathy, provoke the ill feeling they pretend to deprecate, and justify the stern measures resorted to by Congress for the maintenance of national authority.

What Next?

BY THE NEW YORK TIMES | FEB. 22, 1870

The Fifteenth Amendment, ratified on February 3, 1870, established the right of all men to vote regardless of "race, color, or previous condition of servitude."

THE PASSAGE OF the amendment removes from our politics forever a most embarrassing question. It establishes a principle which must always be a part of our Government's policy. As the amendment now stands, it is a sentiment — something expressed, nothing done. We are curious to see what legislation Congress will deem necessary to enforce it.

The application of this amendment to the various conditions under which the franchise has heretofore been granted, in various parts of the country, will be a delicate task. The provisions are exact and intelligible: "The right of citizens of the United States to vote shall not be denied or abridged by the United States, or by any State, on account of race, color, or previous condition of servitude." Under former laws the right of franchise was governed by conflicting qualifications. In Rhode Island the ballot has been subject to an invidious distinction, and the great manufacturing houses, like Brown & Ives, and the Spragues, with their thousands of operatives, virtually controlled the State. In New-York the negro was only permitted to vote when he had a property qualification. In other States he could not vote at all. All this is destroyed by the Amendment. Every man not within the limitation of alienage, or under the ban of the law, or deprived of reason, will stand erect and unchallenged before the ballot!

There will be many efforts to nullify this amendment by restrictive legislation. In Tennessee it is proposed to put a poll tax upon the voters, sufficient to disfranchise at least forty thousand of the freedmen. This may have a temporary effect — as, of course, the black men of Tennessee, or of any Southern State, are poorer than their old masters. We question, however, whether the white men of any Southern State will be willing to tax themselves, merely to gratify their anger against the negro. Legislation of this kind will in time right itself. Establish such a tax, and it adds a stronger motive to the negro to raise himself — to make himself able to pay the tax. It is a stimulus to ambition. It confirms him in his devotion to the party that gave him freedom and citizenship. It prevents the Democracy from gaining any negro votes, and is, in effect, a proposition so absurd that it can never become a precedent.

What limitations, then, are possible under this amendment? There can be no tax that will not injure the white man as much as the negro. There may be a test of naturalization to affect the Chinese — but no party will attempt to pass a law which, while it impedes the Chinamen, also interrupts the Irishman or the German. We cannot make one naturalization law for the yellow men of Asia and another for the white men of Europe. We may say that no heathen — no follower of Buddha — none but those who profess Christianity shall be citizens. It would not surprise us to see such a law attempted in California, but it would be as foolish as the proposed poll tax in Tennessee. If John Chinaman is disenfranchised because he believes in Buddha what shall be done with those of our pale-faced Americans who believe in no God, and have no faith but Reason? It would be difficult to make a law disfranchising the Mongolian that would not embarrass Mr. Emerson or Mr. Robert Dale Owen, and it might even go hard with Mr. Greeley himself. A test of education — and to our mind such a test would be proper — would fall no more heavily upon the negro than upon the white. The constituents of Mackerelville and the Five Points will hesitate before they make a law for Pompey that will in the least embarrass Dermot.

There will be laws and proposed laws to annul and destroy the amendment. Tennessee and Maryland and California and Delaware will probably try to overwhelm this wise and lofty measure with stifling legislation. There can be no law that will be anything more than an annoyance. All that we expect from Congress is certain guarantees that the alien who resides with us shall obey our laws, respect the flag, yield no foreign allegiance, and be in a political sense an American. If Chinamen come merely to make money, that they may go home to their flowery land and spend it they are not citizens, but sojourners! As all of them have this purpose and hope — and live in the daily dream of a return to their loved China, that they there may live and die and mix with its sacred dust — we do not expect many Asiatic accessions to our suffrage. The Chinaman has shown no desire to adopt our customs, our religion, our nationality. He is so much a sojourner that he has not even brought his women. He has shown no desire to make America his home. Until he manifests that desire, we need not look upon him as a serious candidate for the franchise. So in considering the probable workings of this amendment, the Chinese question, which has given so much uneasiness to some of our thinkers, must be considered as adjourned until a new revelation comes over the minds of the Chinese themselves.

The duty of Congress is simple and explicit. Let it enforce this amendment by providing that no laws shall be passed affecting the franchise, except laws that will stimulate education, industry and thrift. Now that we have opened the door to all the children of men to come and sit under our vine and fig tree, and be as essentially American as ourselves, let us strive to encourage them to become worthy of the privilege.

Plain Truths for the Negroes.

BY THE NEW YORK TIMES | SEPT. 24, 1870

THE COLORED PEOPLE have been holding a convention at Poughkeepsie to take into consideration the political and educational interests of their race in three of the Congressional Districts of this State. The President made a very sensible speech, in which he pointed out what the best white friends of the colored people have pointed out frequently since their emancipation, that although their participation in politics is very well as a sign of their equality, and as a means of preserving it, reliance on politics for their social elevation is an immense mistake. He asked very pertinently, "Have they not been hewers of wood and drawers of water long enough? Have they not blacked their master's boots and stood behind his chair until their hearts were sick and sore?" To these questions, we suppose, there can be but one answer; but it is useless, as he also pointed out, for the colored people to expect to escape from their degradation by simply voting. Now that everybody votes, no man is respected for voting any more than for wearing pantaloons, although inability to vote when others did vote would, undoubtedly, be a mark of inferiority. In order to rise in the social scale, the colored race must show itself capable of the acquirements and achievements through which other races have achieved distinction. It must furnish a fair quota of able and successful men of business, of learned and astute lawyers, of well-trained scholars, of eloquent preachers, of painstaking, and clear-headed, and thorough men of science. It must, too, do a reasonable amount for the arts of music and painting, at least — we are disposed in consideration of the multiplicity of white poets to grant it a considerable respite in the matter of poetry. Lastly it must furnish a respectable quota of honorable and polished men of culture, and women of the same sort. It is no doubt pretty hard for a race situated as it has been, and still is, to do all this; but it must be done, in order to attain to anything approaching to social equality. Position in this world is only accorded to desert of some kind, and all the speechifying that could be put into fifty years of conventions would not change the rule. Of course, no race is expected to furnish a great number of first-class men in any department, but it has to furnish some, and of their performances the race gets the benefit in respect and reputation.

But, then, at the bottom of all social improvement is improvement in character. Without a good basis of truthful, manly, self-reliant, upright character, there is no use in the colored people trying to raise themselves socially in the estimation of their white neighbors, and they may depend upon it that if they are going to act on the first resolution adopted by the Convention, they will not hasten the formation of that type of character, or any other type that will be of use either to them or to the community at large. That resolution was, "That this Convention will discountenance any person or persons who has or will continue to vote the Democratic ticket, and that we agree to disregard them, and will not give any place or protection or shelter or in houses or places of business, but consider them an enemy to our race forever." The grammar of this is not encouraging, though if this were its only defect it would pass well enough. But the colored people could hardly hit on a better mode of keeping themselves down, and making themselves both contemptible and ridiculous, than by a formal attempt to use their social intercourse as a means of political proscription. Moreover, they could hardly hit on a better mode of cultivating meanness, deceit, and other small vices, which sap character just as effectively as the great ones, and the prevalence of which has already a good deal to do with their degradation. The resolution, too, stands in extraordinary contrast with the advice of the President and the avowed objects of the Convention, both of which urge reliance on self-culture, through education and other ways, as the sole means of regeneration. We are no friends of the Democratic Party, and we believe the colored people, like the Irish, and indeed the poor and ignorant of all races, have no worse enemy than this same party; but, then, a negro, who is kept from voting for it, by the fear that he would lose his place, or be cut off from social intercourse with his friends, would be a contemptible fellow, and sure to make a bad Republican. The same thing might he said of the negroes who watched him and persecuted him.

Of course the professional politicians on both sides are ready enough to work the colored people up into furies of this kind, but the professional politicians are sorry guides for any race which has a social education to acquire. We see the Poughkeepsie Convention is going to take measures to have "the strength of the colored people ascertained, in the three Congressional districts," which is very well as long as they don't flatter themselves that "their strength" lies in their numbers. Their real strength must always be in their education, or in other words in their ability, to see where, in politics as in other things, their real interests lie, and to avoid falling into the hands of, and being led blindfold by, white demagogues. For which reason, we anticipate a great deal more good from the determination of the Convention "to build an academy, seminary, or high school," in or near Poughkeepsie, than from its determination to have "the colored vote brought out" in those districts.

The attempts of the colored people to work their way up have not thus far been very fortunate. They have by no means put their best men into the front rank. They have sent one or two men to the Bar here at the North, who have been miserable failures in every way; and though some of their leaders at the South have been good men, their politicians have, on the whole, done them no credit. Their cadets, too, at West Point have certainly not been selected in such a way as to assert the principle of equality with much honor, and one or two mistakes, such as the election of Whittemore, have disheartened a good many of their friends. But they have distinguished students now both at Yale and Harvard, and there are plenty of other signs that, with good sense and hard work, there is nothing to hinder them from winning, if not a place in the very front rank, still a very respectable place.

Woman's Rights and the Fashions — A Rebuke from "Sojourner Truth."

BY THE NEW YORK TIMES | NOV. 3, 1870

DURING THE WOMANS' RIGHTS gathering at Providence, R. I., the old colored woman, Sojourner Truth, made the following remarks on the fashions and foibles of the age:

"I'm awful hard on dress, you know. Women, you forgot that you are the mothers of creation; you forgot your sons were cut off like grass by the war, and the land was covered with their blood; you rig yourselves up in panniers Grecian bend backs and flummeries; yes, and mothers and gray-haired grandmothers wear high-heeled shoes and humps on their heads, and put them on their babies, and stuff them out so that they keel over when the wind blows. Oh, mothers, I'm ashamed of ye! What will such lives as you do for humanity? When I saw them women on the stage at the Women's Suffrage Convention the other day, I thought, what kind of reformers be you, with goose wings on your heads, as if you were going to fly, and dressed in such ridiculous fashion, talking about reform and women's rights? 'Pears to me you had better reform yourselves first. But Sojourner is an old body, and will soon go out of this world into another, and wants to say when she gets there, 'Lord, I have done my duty, I have told the whole truth and kept nothing back.' "

Louisiana's Separate Car Law.

BY THE NEW YORK TIMES | MAY 19, 1896

WASHINGTON, MAY 18 — The Supreme Court to-day, in an opinion read by Justice Brown, sustained the constitutionality of the law of Louisiana requiring the railroads of the State to provide separate cars for white and colored passengers. There was no inter-State commerce feature in the case, for the railroad upon which the incident occurred giving rise to the case — Plessy vs. Ferguson — the East Louisiana Railroad — was and is operated wholly within the State. The opinion states that by analogy to the laws of Congress and of many of the States requiring the establishment of separate schools for children of the two races, and other similar laws, the statute in question was within the competency of the Louisiana Legislature, exercising the police power of the State. The judgement of the Supreme Court of the State, upholding the law, was therefore affirmed.

Mr. Justice Harlan announced a very vigorous dissent, saying that he saw nothing but mischief in all such laws. In his view of the case, no power in the land had the right to regulate the enjoyment of the civil rights upon the basis of race. It would be just as reasonable and proper, he said, for States to pass laws requiring separate cars to be furnished for Catholics and Protestants, or for descendants of those of the Teutonic race and those of the Latin race.

CHAPTER 2

The Promise
of Equality

People of color had the legal right to freedom, citizenship, employment and fair wages. But discriminatory laws and practices prevented many people from employing these rights. Activists held conferences on race. Some advocated industrial education as a way to improve people's lives. Others proposed more assertive methods such as going on strike. The highly controversial film "The Birth of a Nation" was released and protested. And thirty years later, the federal government imprisoned Japanese-Americans for the duration of World War II.

Race Problem Conference; Speakers at Montgomery Discuss Lynching; Extermination of Blacks Said to Be Inevitable

BY THE NEW YORK TIMES | MAY 11, 1900

MONTGOMERY, ALA., MAY 10 — At the morning session of the Race Conference the discussion centred about the negro in relation to religion.

Prof. John Roachstraton of Mercer University, Mason; the Rev. D. Clay Lilley of Tuscaloosa, Secretary of the Southern Presbyterian Board of Negro Evangelization; and W. A. Guerry, Chaplain of the University of the South, took part in the discussion. The Rev. C. C. Brown or Clinton, S. C. and the Very Rev. J. R. Slattery of Baltimore, spoke for the advisability of raising the standard of ordination.

Bishop Rennick of Baltimore declared, that from five to eight negroes in the North under Northern conditions committed crimes to one in the South. Prof. W. F. Willcox, Statistician in the Census Bureau, declared that the ultimate extermination of the black race was inevitable. "There will be a rapid decrease of the birth rate and a slow increase of the death rate until the negro race will stand as the American Indian stands to-day," said Prof. Willcox.

Prof. Willcox was followed by Secretary Herbert Welsh of the Indian Rights Association. At the afternoon session Alex C. King of Atlanta opened the discussion of the lynching question. He spoke on "The Punishment of Crimes Against Women — Existing Legal Remedies and Their Sufficiency."

Mr. King said it was in those communities where the dominance of the white race was the least secure and the menace of the black criminal the greatest that lynch law is most likely to prevail. He called attention to the fact that with the passage of time since the abolition of slavery the crime seems to grow in importance. Mr. King also noted the apparently inherent prejudice existing between the lower class of white people and the negro, who, in being educated and by imitation, was menacing the social status of this class of white people. He said that this prejudice is resented by the negro and produces strong racial animosity.

Mr. King gave two reasons why extra judicial means are resorted to, namely, the delay of legal punishment and the protection of the victim of the assault from the ordeal of the witness chair. He suggested two remedies for mob violence. He thought that when a party begins a hunt for a fugitive each member should be sworn in as a Deputy Sheriff by the Sheriff of the county and a memorandum of his name taken. In case violence came to the prisoner, those committing it could be detected. He also suggested that for every county where a lynching occurred a tax should be levied by the State authorities of not less than $5,000 and the amount appropriated to the School Fund of the State. He closed with a plea for the domination of law.

He was followed by Clifton R. Breckinridge of Arkansas, who discussed the advisability of lynching.

W. Bourke Cockran of New York boldly advocated the repeal of the Fifteenth Amendment to the Federal Constitution. He argued that it was a bad limb on the tree; that it had been nullified by the States; that it had been lynched, so to speak, by the people of the South.

He declared that the reconciliation of the theoretical status of the negro under the Constitution should be reconciliation with his actual status in the public opinion of the country. He maintained that this repeal was best for the negro as well as for the white man, since both races had to live together, to prosper together, or go down together. Every source of irritation between the two should be removed, and the Fifteenth Amendment was the greatest.

Mr. Cockran asserted that the path of the negro to political and social rights lay through the development of the unit, the individual, and that the only means was by industrial education.

Is the Turk a White Man?

BY THE NEW YORK TIMES | SEPT. 30, 1909

THE AMERICAN COURTS have barred from citizenship Chinese, Japanese, Burmese, and their half-breeds. Will they bar Turks? The United States Circuit Court in Cincinnati has been called upon to decide whether a Turkish citizen shall be naturalized as a white person. Only "to aliens being free white persons, and to aliens of African nativity and to persons of African descent," does the statute admitting to American citizenship apply. Few Turks migrate to this country, fewer settle here. But this case is of interest to the representatives of the Hunnish and Magyar peoples, whose stock is akin to the Turks, and who constitute a chief part of our immigrants. The original Turks were of the yellow or Mongolian race. Timur and his Turkish-speaking descendants founded the Mogol or Mongol Empire in India. Jenghiz Khan, a Mongolian, headed the invasions into Russia with hordes of Turkish-speaking soldiery, of Tartar or Manchu stock, from the central and western steppes of Asia. They swept down into Persia, overran Arabia and Egypt, and invaded Europe to Vienna. Before them came the plundering Huns, or Hiung-nu, as they were known in China.

But in their westward progress the Turks freely intermingled with the Caucasian races whom they subjugated. The Turks in Constantinople to-day are the descendants of Arabs, Kurds, Slavs, Albanians, and Greeks, and of foreign slave girls of more mixed ancestry. The deposed Abdul shows unmistakably Semitic features. But Sir Charles Eliot would not generalize from the physique of the Turks of Constantinople. In his book on "Turkey in Europe" he says:

> In June, 1897, I saw many thousand Turkish soldiers together in Thessaly, collected from all parts of Anatolia, and was much impressed by the strongly non-Caucasian type of many.

And President George Washburn of Robert College has testified:

The Turkish mind does not work as ours, and it is very difficult, even for one who has lived in Constantinople for fifty years in close relations with the people, to predict from one day to another what is likely to happen.

They are a cruel and massacring people, and they have lost none of their ancient proclivities. But they are also Europeans, as much "white" people as the Huns, Finns, and Cossacks. A trace of negro blood, if only enough to stain the fingers about the nails, will bar a person from white society. But that is a distinction chiefly of caste, not really of race. Would so narrow a distinction, or even a broader one, prevent the Turk from being considered a white man?

Socialist Advises Negroes to Strike

BY THE NEW YORK TIMES | MAY 13, 1910

Speech by Clarence Darrow stirs sociologists in Cooper Union to warm protest. He told the negroes that mob law was about as just as the courts, and scoffed at their industrial progress.

THE EFFORTS WHICH the National Negro Committee, including in its membership many of the most prominent clergymen and sociologists of this city, made yesterday afternoon and evening to urge the negroes of this country to develop themselves through industrial education, were rudely interrupted in the conference's session last night in Cooper Union.

Clarence Darrow, who was counsel for Moyer, Heywood, and Pettibone, the Colorado dynamiters, did the interrupting. When it came to be his turn to speak, Mr. Darrow coolly advised the seven or eight hundred negroes who had crowded into Copper Union to hear the speeches that the best way for them to better their condition in the South and throughout the country was to "stop working."

"What the South wants by its acts of disenfranchisement is not to make the negro leave the South, but to make the negro keep his place," Darrow told the negroes. "The reason that the South aids your industrial schools is so that the negro may be taught to lay bricks better — for the benefit of the white man.

"If I were going to advise the negroes of this country what to do, I would advise them to follow the example of the whites and get along without working. Why do you go to the industrial schools? Do you want more work? Why should you want it? You won't get more wages for it. The whites won't give you any more wages. They don't give more wages to horses."

At another point in his address Mr. Darrow told the negroes that "mob law is more expeditious than court law, and it's a question whether it isn't about as just."

These and other remarks by Mr. Darrow were received with

The attorney Clarence Darrow, circa 1915.

increasing whoops of laughter from the younger of the 800 negroes and with blinking surprise by the older and more staid. To the clergymen and sociologists on the platform, however, many of whom had in speeches immediately preceding Mr. Darrow's advised the negroes that the solution of the race problem would come about gradually if both races were patient and tried to learn to understand each other, this new tone was in the nature of a bombshell.

SPEECHES IN A DIFFERENT NOTE.

The meeting followed an afternoon conference of the Negro Committee in the Charity Organization Society's Mall. The Rev. Percy Stickney Grant presided at the evening meeting, and there were speeches by many prominent folk, including Ray Stannard Baker, the Rev. R. C. Ransom, pastor of the Bethel A. M. E. Church, and Mrs. Ida Wells-Barnett, the colored sociologist, whose investigations and public pleadings caused Gov. Deneen of Illinois to remove Sheriff Frank E. Davis of Alexander

County for neglect of duty after the Cairo lynchings last November.

"Dr. Grant had pointed out to the negro audience that the "purpose of life is the progressive development of every human being. "And Mrs. Wells-Barnett, by a vivid description of the lynching of Will James in Cairo last November had shown the horrors of the mob law which Mr. Darrow subsequently said was "about as just as the law of the courts."

"The lynching of Will James in the streets of Cairo, Ill., on last Nov. 11 was the most inhuman spectacle which has ever been seen in this country," said Mrs. Wells-Barnett. "A white girl had been found murdered and bloodhounds followed a scent to a house three blocks away.

"Will James happened to be staying in that house, and the gag in the girl's mouth was of the same texture as the girl's clothes. Sheriff Davis, without swearing in Deputies or appealing to the town's two companies of militia, arrested James and took him twenty-five miles out of town. There, the pursuing mob dragged James off the train.

"They took him back to Cairo and hanged him to a steel arch in Washington Street with a rope. The rope broke and they riddled his body with bullets. Then they dragged it a mile up Washington Street in the dust, burned it, and stuck the head on a fence picket. Then they went to the jail and lynched Salzner, a white man. Sheriff Davis, whom Gov. Deneen afterward removed, did not provide himself with adequate guards to interfere."

It was after Mrs. Wells-Barnett's speech that the Rev. Dr. Grant introduced Mr. Darrow as the "champion of the unprivileged classes." Mr. Darrow began his speech by telling the 700 negroes jocularly that "the older he grew the less he believed in voting."

"The world, so far, has failed to prove that it can vote itself into any condition that is worth while," he remarked, while the clergymen and reformers on the stage began to straighten themselves in their chairs and blink in astonishment. "As a of matter of fact, the good cause which Sumner and Phillips fought so bravely for fifty years ago is dead. A black man has been lynched, almost in the shadow of the statue of Abraham Lincoln in the town that Lincoln lived in. No Horace

Greeley wrote or spoke against it. Our most talented men, nowadays, use their brains and voices merely to help the corporations rob the poor. Step by step the South has reconquered the North.

"The negroes are being crucified because the Lord made them black. Only one thing have they gained. They have industrial schools — industrial schools in which they are taught better to lay brick for the white man. What the negro needs is not more work but more wages. The North itself no longer believes in the equality of the negro. As for my own beliefs, I can say that mob law is more expeditious, and it is a great question whether it is not just as often right as the slower-moving law of the courts.

"I wouldn't have laid a hand on that mob in Springfield, but if we are going to lynch the blacks we must also lynch the whites. Now the leader of the black race runs up a white flag at Atlanta and says: 'We don't want social equality.' What do you want — more work?

"Why aren't you entitled to social equality? Your race contains many famous men. You have Dumas, Tuissaint, L'Ouverture, Fred Douglass, Booker Washington, Prof. Du Bois, "Jack" Johnson. It's false philosophy that teaches the negro that he can get along all right without the ballot so long as he is allowed to put a dollar in a bank."

"The laws don't go far enough in protecting everybody.

"Back of the acts of the Cairo and Springfield mobs is prejudice — the prejudice built up by the clergymen in the pulpits and the lawyers in the courts, pleading the causes of the rich. The whites hate the negroes because the negroes carry on their faces the badge of slavery. The race question is, at bottom, a labor question. A man who works is not allowed to associate with a man who doesn't work. Pretty soon, a man who works will be obliged to leave his voting to the idle.

"You negroes should stop working — stop working and amalgamate yourselves with the white working classes. Learn to use your votes so as to help yourselves. And stop taking tips from white men."

THE REV. PERCY GRANT STOPS HIM.

All this time there had been increasing whoops from the younger negroes in the audience and increasing silence and embarrassment among the philanthropists on the platform. At the statement that "the clergy in the pulpit are pleading the cause of the rich," the Rev. Percy Stickney Grant had started visibly and through the rest of the Western lawyer's address had sat with a frozen smile and a crimson face. When Mr. Darrow reached the point where he began advising the negroes not to take tips, the clergyman-Chairman arose and, very red, tiptoed across the big platform, and, taking Darrow by the right arm, whispered a short and earnest sentence in his ear.

Mr. Darrow immediately broke off his speech and walked back to his seat on the platform. In introducing Congressman Bennet, the next speaker, the Chairman, still very red, made no reference at all to Mr. Darrow's speech.

"I want to disagree with Mr. Darrow at the very start," said Congressman Bennet. "I don't approve of lynching at all. I think that when Mr. Darrow said that he wouldn't have laid a hand on that mob in Springfield, he was quite wrong. I spent my boyhood in the only town in New York State in which there ever was a lynching. Before the lynching the blacks and whites lived together in perfect harmony. I had many negro friends. After the lynching all was different."

In introducing the Rev. R. C. Ranson, the colored pastor of the Bethel A.M.E. Church, Dr. Grant, with a grim smile, remarked:

"Unfortunately, it would seem, in view of certain of the remarks which have been made on this platform to-night, I now seem to have the honor of introducing the pastor of an aristocratic pulpit, of an aristocratic church, where an aristocratic congregation are taught how to get to an aristocratic heaven."

Neither the Rev. Dr. Grant nor Congressman Bennet would comment on Mr. Darrow's speech after the meeting.

Written on the Screen

BY THE NEW YORK TIMES | FEB. 27, 1915

D W. GRIFFITH'S spectacular film production, "The Birth of a Nation," will be given its first public exhibition Wednesday night in the Liberty Theatre. The scenario is based on Thomas Dixon's novel and play "The Clansman," while the film is exhibited to the accompaniment of special music written by Joseph Carl Briel, composer of the music of "The Climax," and played by a symphony orchestra of forty musicians.

The story begins in the seventeenth century with the coming of the first African slaves to North America. The civil war is pictured in some of its most striking details. Sherman's march to the sea, the burning of Atlanta, the fall of Petersburgh, the surrender of Lee at Appomattox, and the assassination of Lincoln are some of the episodes shown.

Eight months were taken in making the picture, which is said to be one of the most elaborate ever produced. There are 18,000 people and 3,000 horses in its many scenes.

A Woman's Protest

LETTER | THE NEW YORK TIMES | MARCH 21, 1915

TO THE EDITOR OF THE NEW YORK TIMES:

I wish to voice my protest against the second part of the moving-picture film entitled "The Birth of a Nation" presented at the Liberty Theatre. The portrayal, unjust as it is to the negro, showing him as a cruel, inhuman, almost demented being, cannot help but create prejudice against a race that has a difficult road to travel at best and needs all possible sympathy and understanding from his white neighbor.

Furthermore, the film presents a biased point of view that over-emphasizes the mistakes of reconstruction days (in regard to carpet-baggers and their influence on negroes) on the one hand and glorifies the Ku-klux Klan on the other (the latter is portrayed as constantly rescuing defenseless maidens from the outrageous hands of the colored man). Thus it rouses the feelings of resentment and hatred that almost shattered our country a half century ago.

At the present date, when the nations across the sea are at each other's throats, when the worst passions of men are unleashed, this film is particularly untimely. It is particularly dangerous to open up old wounds and stir up prejudices of long ago.

I believe it is possible to have moving pictures dramatic and interesting without resorting to portrayals of this sort that are unjust and only half true to history.

ANNETTE WALLACH ERDMANN, NEW YORK.

Negroes Mob Photo Play.

BY THE NEW YORK TIMES | APRIL 18, 1915

BOSTON, APRIL 17 — The trouble threatened ever since the photo play "The Birth of a Nation" began its engagement at the Tremont Theater culminated tonight when 500 negroes, headed by W. Munroe Trotter, who made what was called an insulting address to President Wilson at the White House not long ago, arrived in a body and tried to buy tickets. The management declared that the house was sold out and that the people who were getting tickets at the box office had purchased them in advance. Trotter and his friends, among whom were several white men, assumed such an attitude that Manager Schoeffel called in the police, and a squad of 100, headed by Superintendent Crowley in person, hurried to the theater in automobiles.

The lobby was cleared without the use of clubs and the performance proceeded. In the audience were several negroes who had purchased seats in advance.

Six arrests were made — Trotter, the Rev. A. W. Fuller, pastor of the People's Baptist Church, John Hines, and two other negroes, and Joseph Gould, a white man.

Bar Negro Women's Vote.

BY THE NEW YORK TIMES | NOV. 3, 1920

SAVANNAH, GA., NOV. 2 — Ballots were refused negro women at the voting places in Savannah today. Many negro women had registered since the suffrage amendment became effective, but the election judges ruled they were not entitled to vote because of a State law which requires registration six months before an election.

No white women presented themselves at the polls.

Better Relations Between Races Sought At a Student Conference in the South

BY THE NEW YORK TIMES | JULY 20, 1930

ATLANTA, GA., JULY 16 — At the recent Southern Student Y.M.C.A. Conference held at Blue Ridge, N. C., the race relations group decided that something should be done to promote better relations between white and Negro students, and that the races should cooperate.

To start such a movement the group drew up resolutions which were discussed and passed, although not unanimously. The resolutions took cognizance of "the difficulties under which the Negro operates to-day;" pledged the conference to seek a better understanding of the Negro student and placed the white students on record as seeking a "fair deal" for the black race. The resolutions recommended to the Southern field council that an interconference retreat for a limited number of students from both the Kings Mountain and the Blue Ridge conferences be again undertaken, and that this conference record itself as favoring the entertainment of its invited guests "on the same basis."

It is doubtful if any other meeting of whites in the South has passed resolutions so free from any suggestion of race prejudice or more earnestly expressing a desire to be helpful to the Negro. Present at the conference from this State were students from the University of Georgia, Emory University at Atlanta, the Berry Schools of Rome, Georgia Tech, Atlanta, and Piedmont College, Demorest, Ga.

New Racial Ideas Taught

BY THE NEW YORK TIMES | MAY 20, 1934

SYMPATHETIC ATTITUDES between children of different races are being developed among pupils through special programs in the junior and senior high schools of Englewood, N. J. The work is part of a movement to improve racial relations in the United States which is being promoted by the recently organized Service Bureau for Education in Human Relations of 519 West 121st Street. The methods used are the outgrowth of seven years of experimentation in various schools. Many prominent educators in New York and other centres are members of a national committee sponsoring the bureau.

These programs at Englewood take simple forms and follow one of three lines. That is, they take one of these three main approaches toward the development of desired attitudes: the intellectual, which means the giving of facts about the various cultural groups; the emotional, which seeks to stir the feelings; and the situational, which means the arrangement of situations — as natural as possible — in which the students may act out the new attitude.

APPEAL TO THE EMOTIONS.

The most striking, of course, is the emotional approach. This is made by having children of one racial group entertain the school assembly with a play or tableaux or program combining various dramatic appeals. Such presentations, used especially in the junior high school, take some characteristic custom of a race, or some particular contribution to history or American life, or a series of such contributions, and bring out their importance, their background, or perhaps merely their charm.

On one occasion, for example, students of one racial group came from New York, together with a party of school friends of what might be called unclassified races. They gave a program combining a play, an interpretative dance and a talk, which showed the charm of some of the traditions of that race and its many-sided contacts with American life.

A visit of this kind gives a splendid opportunity for the situational approach. For this purpose the "home rooms" are used; that is, the rooms in which the students make their headquarters for the school day. After an assembly program by a visiting group, the students of one home room entertain the party at tea together with delegates from other home rooms and outside community organizations.

This leads into the intellectual approach in one of its chief forms. In the week following such an assembly program, discussions are held in all home rooms throughout the school, about the particular racial group that was represented.

A second method of intellectual approach is the assembly talk by a member of one of the racial minorities prominent in his community. Such talks are used especially at the senior high school assemblies. They have at times aroused so much interest that, after a one-hour talk, students have remained a second hour asking questions. The literature and history sections of the school follow the talks with assigned units of study on the questions raised.

GROWTH OF ASSEMBLY PROGRAMS.

The value of such work has been demonstrated in the previous experimentation, carried on in schools from Washington, D. C., to Boston. The initial work was with assembly programs in the high school at Woodbury, N. J., where the plan of having a series built around one idea was used.

After three years of consciously trying to develop more tolerant attitudes toward other races and nations we gave our seniors the Neumann attitude test and found them to be on the average 22 points more tolerant than a similar group of students from a near-by school.

This test asks students to pass on the truth of such questions as, "The people of the white race are born mentally superior to the other races such as the yellow peoples of China and Japan, the black peoples of Africa, the North American Indians, the people of India," and, "The white people dominate the black and brown races because the white people are naturally more clever than the black and brown peoples can ever be."

Our bureau provides supplementary materials for classroom and home-room discussions, as well as suggestions for the dramatic assembly programs. This material is not to be found now to any extent in the usual texts or reference books. On the contrary, in a typical school library studied in detail we found 560 lines which would produce antagonistic attitudes toward one race or another.

The bureau is publishing a series of books for high schools providing selected readings on the following groups: the British, Scandinavian; Far Eastern, Mexican and South American, Jewish, Slavic, Teutonic, Negro, Near Eastern and Latin. The bureau also assists in connecting the school with outstanding community leaders and organizations representing the different culture groups.

The chairman of the bureau is Dr. Heber Harper of Teachers College, Columbia University, Dr. Otis W. Caldwell of Columbia is treasurer and Dr. F. Tredwell Smith research secretary.

West Coast Moves to Oust Japanese

BY LAWRENCE E. DAVIES | JAN. 29, 1942

SAN FRANCISCO, JAN. 28 — An anti-fifth column campaign aimed at rid-
ding State and city payrolls of all persons of Japanese ancestry, even
though they themselves are American citizens, and moving all Japanese nationals to internment camps or at least out of the coastal war
zone, made progress today on several fronts.

Mayor Bowron of Los Angeles annnounced that all of the American-
born Japanese on that city's payrolls had been "permitted" to apply
for a leave of absence. This means that thirty-nine have severed their
connections with the city's service for the duration of the war.

The action of the Los Angeles city departments followed the dismissal of fifty-six American-Japanese employees of county offices by
the Los Angeles board of supervisors, who requested President Roosevelt and Federal officials to move some 13,000 Japanese aliens from
defense areas to inland farm districts.

"We just felt," Mayor Bowron said, "that for the safety of the city it
was best to remove all employes with Japanese connections. Many of
them had access to important city records, maps end other valuable
documents."

Reports from Washington that the Navy needed Terminal Island,
home of a Japanese colony of 2,100 including 800 aliens at Los Angeles,
was regarded as a possible answer to the requests that this strategic
tract be cleared of Orientals.

The Los Angeles action was applauded by Dan Gallagher, acting
president of the San Francisco Board of Supervisors, who said that he
had been planning to introduce a resolution at next Monday's meeting
of the local board dealing with the Japanese question.

He said that "the Mayor ought to put an embargo on truck garden
produce brought in here by Japanese. Everything can be taken care of
here by our own truck gardeners."

Upholds Japanese in Citizens' Right

BY LAWRENCE E. DAVIES | FEB. 21, 1943

SAN FRANCISCO. FEB. 20 — Without leaving the bench, seven judges of the Ninth Federal Circuit Court of Appeals blocked to-day a move to deprive 70,000 evacuated Japanese-Americans of their citizenship.

U. S. Webb, former State Attorney General, arguing the case on behalf of John T. Regan, secretary of The Native Sons of the Golden West, inferentially asked the court to rule contrary to the decision of the Supreme Court in the Wong Kim case of 1898. That decision, upholding the citizenship of a Chinese born in this country, has been accepted as applying to American-born Japanese as well.

Mr. Webb told the court that "without committing treason" he believed that that case was "erroneously decided."

"Are you asking this court to overrule a decision of the Supreme Court," Judge Curtis D. Wilbur, senior member of the court, asked.

"I'm asking the court, as God gives it light and power, to give a correct judgment according to law," the attorney responded. "I am aware that you have sworn to uphold the Constitution, but I am not aware that you have sworn to follow decisions of the Supreme Court whether they are right or wrong in your judgment."

When Mr. Webb asserted that the country had been settled and the governments organized by whites, Judge Denman asked:

"How about the Indians?"

The attorney admitted that "ethnologically speaking" there was a theory that "in the misty past" the Mongolian had been an ancestor of the Indian, whereupon the same judge demanded:

"Do you know anybody who disputes it?"

"I contend," Mr. Webb, replied, "that the American Indian is not an Asiatic."

Without hearing argument by opposing counsel. Judge Wilbur announced that the judgment of the lower court, throwing out the

Native Sons' petition to have names of Japanese-Americans stricken from the voting lists, would be affirmed.

The court listened to argument, uncompleted at an all-day session yesterday, on the constitutionality of President Roosevelt's Executive Order 9066 and subsequent proclamations of Lieut. Gen. Dewitt, Western defense commander, authorizing and executing the evacuation of the West Coast Japanese. Edward. J. Ennis, a special assistant attorney general, was asked by Judge Denman whether there was "a single case from Pearl Harbor to the evacuation" wherein one of the 70,000 American-born Japanese had been "found by competent authority to be a menace."

Mr. Ennis said he knew of none, but that "incalculable damage" could have been done "even if only few hundred" of them had been hostile in the event of an attempted invasion of this coast.

Fifty Years of Crusading for the Negro in America

REVIEW | BY LOMBARD C. JONES | DEC. 22, 1940

Dusk of Dawn: An Essay Toward an Autobiography of a Race Concept.
W. E. Burghardt Du Bois. 334 pp. New York: Harcourt, Brace & Co. $2.

WHEN DR. DU BOIS began this book it was his intention to record the sense of dawning victory that he has come to feel after fifty years of valorous crusading for the rights of American Negroes. A seventieth birthday, however, pressed him to expand the original pattern; remarks and comments on a long and stubbornly fought battle seemed called for. The result — "Dusk of Dawn" with its appropriate but mouth-filling subtitle — traces sensitively and with vital force a progression of life and thought dedicated to what this great Negro leader believes is the central problem of our democracy and of the future world.

Du Bois grew up in the tolerant, provincial atmosphere of Great Barrington, a town of Western Massachusetts which, in the Seventies and early Eighties, numbered no more than fifty Negroes among its 5,000 inhabitants. His mother's family, among whom he was raised, had lived in the shadow of its hills for generations. Their social status, relatively humble in the community, was determined by income and ancestry more than by color. Because of this economic leveling and his own keen sensitiveness and pride, Du Bois did not realize the shackling force of racial discrimination until he had left New England with a scholarship in his pocket to attend college in the South.

At Fisk University, Nashville, Tenn., studying and teaching among people of his own color, Du Bois learned new things about the world — things like "Jim Crow" cars, public disdain and insult for Negroes encountered on the street, the violence of rope and pistol, lynch law and its sadistic enforcement. He came to question the white world's interpretation of democratic development and to wonder how the American Negro, particularly in the South, could be admitted to open and effective participation in the "inevitable and logical democracy."

After his graduation from Fisk in 1888 a succession of scholarships enabled him to continue his education at Harvard. There, under the wise tutelage of William James, he turned from philosophy to history and social science, and continued with unabated zeal his study of the Negro problem in America. His doctor's thesis, "The Suppression of the Slave Trade," became the first volume in the Harvard Historical Studies.

In 1892 Du Bois went abroad on a fellowship granted by the Slater Fund for the education of Negroes. Two years spent in traveling about Europe and in studying at the University of Berlin convinced him that race problems in America, in Africa and in Asia tied into the same vicious circle — a circle of economic exploitation dominated by political action in Europe.

At 26, his formal education completed, he came home to look for a job. He found one eventually: teaching classics at Wilberforce University, Ohio; salary, $800 a year. He continued teaching for sixteen years — at Wilberforce, at the University of Pennsylvania, and at Atlanta University. It was at Atlanta that he produced his monumental series of studies of the American Negro, covering Negro mortality, urbanization, efforts among Negroes for social betterment, Negroes in business, the Negro common school, the Negro church, Negro crime, the health and physique of Negroes, and related subjects.

It was at Atlanta also that the controversy between Du Bois and Booker T. Washington developed. It began as a difference in ideologies. Du Bois believed in the education of a "Talented Tenth" among American Negroes, who would lead their people to a better and more privileged life. Washington was content to put the emphasis on training in the skilled trades, on encouragement in industry and common labor. He minimized the importance of higher education.

Beyond this cleavage in ideals, however, lay the rise of what Dr. Du Bois chooses to call the Tuskegee Machine. Briefly, he contends that, as the distinguished head of Tuskegee Institute, Booker Washington failed in his leadership of American Negroes by emphasizing the shortcomings of his race at a time when the South was passing dis-franchising and "Jim Crow" laws, that Washington's attitude toward higher education for Negroes endeared him to Northern white philan-thropists who did not propose to have their charities responsible for educating to discontent a strong black labor force with which they hoped to check the demands of white labor. According to Du Bois, no Negro institution could collect funds without Washington's consent, and his opposition could be fatal to the careers of aspiring young col-ored men who failed to toe his line.

Out of this controversy grew the Niagara Movement, significantly championing, among other things, freedom of speech and criticism, the recognition of the highest and best human training as the monopoly of no caste or race, full manhood suffrage, a belief in the dignity of labor, and a united effort to realize such ideate under wise and courageous leadership. In 1909 the Niagara Movement was absorbed by a new and larger organization, the National Association for the Advancement of Colored People, of which Dr. Du Bois became director of publications and research. In 1910 his idea of a critical periodical for the American Negro came to fruition in the first issue of the association's organ of propaganda and defense, The Crisis, whose pages under his editorship have borne the first published work of many distinguished contempo-rary Negro writers.

During the World War Du Bois conducted a successful fight to have Negro officers trained and put in command of Negro troops. Immedi-ately after the armistice the N.A.A.C.P. sent him to France to investi-gate the treatment of Negro soldiers and to record their chapter in the history of the conflict. While there, he conceived of and called to meet-ing the Pan-African Congress, the main purpose of which was to have Negroes of the world represented at the Peace Congress. Back home again, he led the N.A.A.C.P's fight against lynching, a fight lost on the Senate floor in 1924 with the defeat of the Dyer Anti-Lynching Bill.

"It was not until years after that I knew what killed that anti-lynching bill," he writes. "It was a bargain between the South and West.

Portrait of W. E. Burghardt Du Bois by artist Frank Walts on the cover of "The Crisis."

By this bargain, lynching was let to go on uncurbed by Federal law, on condition that the Japanese be excluded from the United States."

Of communism in the United States and its meddling with the Scottsboro case he is contemptuous. "With quiet and careful methods," he declares, "the Scottsboro victims would have been freed …. But in the case of the Communists the actual fate of these victims was a minor matter." For the accomplishments of communism in Russia, however, in compelling the world to face problems hitherto avoided, he has unstinted admiration, though by no means does he condone its defections.

This is but a bare outline of a career bristling with activity in the furtherance of a single cause. Its compelling force, its philosophy, are to be found in two chapters — "The White World" and "The Colored World Within." They contain as frank and complete statements of the Negroes' grievances and of proposals advocated for their correction as one could wish to find. They alone are worth the concentrated attention of those intellectuals who believe that our internal problems are minimal, that they can be easily solved, and that we are sufficiently advanced in their solution to advertise our own special brand of social and economic cure-all on the battered hoardings of the outside world.

How to Prevent Riots

OPINION | THE NEW YORK TIMES | AUG. 17, 1943

ONE HUNDRED AND THIRTY-EIGHT good American names, representing many racial origins, religions, occupations and points of view, are signed to an appeal made public this week by Dr. William Allan Neilson, president emeritus of Smith College. The signers are deeply concerned over the situation which produced race riots in Detroit and other communities. Such riots, as they say, embody "many of the practices which have been associated with Nazi Germany and her partner, the Japanese Empire." Unchecked, the tendencies which they represent "threaten the very foundation of the Republic itself."

Dr. Neilson's committee is absolutely right. There could be no race riots if a good many citizens did not hold to the vicious doctrine of superior and inferior races. And there will be no American democracy if this contagion of ignorance, foolishness and fear ever infects a majority of us. Of course it won't ever do that. The danger is that a small nitwit minority will have its way at times and do great harm because the sane and well-meaning majority is also too easy-going.

It is the obligation of the citizen to know what his principles are and to stand up for them. It is not sufficient to stand up for them after the rioting begins. They must be defended by words and acts in the round of everyday life. We have to have courage to rebuke intolerance when it shows itself. We have to have good-will and a sense of fair play ready for use in subways, elevators and factories, in the humdrum matters of daily life. Intolerance is always explicit and dramatic. Why not put a little drama into the role of being a good neighbor?

Move to Curb Racial Strife

LETTER | BY THE NEW YORK TIMES | AUG. 20, 1943

TO THE EDITOR OF THE NEW YORK TIMES:

Your editorial, "How to Prevent Race Riots," contains some very timely words in these days of excitement. In line with your statements, there is a movement which has been growing to national scope for nearly a year to forestall and to ease the tensions and conflicts that close observers have expected. This movement, sponsored by the Federal Council of Churches and allied agencies, is helping "To End This Day of Strife" by enlisting for interracial brotherhood the active, courageous service of individuals in the local community.

Each individual is asked to declare his decision:

1. "To act positively and constructively wherever racial tensions can be corrected and interracial justice and good-will advanced.

2. To seek fellowship with others who are like-minded and to work with them wherever mutually agreeable.

3. To become informed about the facts of race relations, especially the phases that affect me and others of my community in our daily living.

4. To seek Divine guidance and vision for carrying out these intentions."

The primary aim of this declaration is to recruit a larger number of people from different walks of life and different racial groups in the local community "to become well informed and active instead of passive spectators in the struggle for interracial justice and good-will" within the scope of each person's daily living in his work, home, church or synagogue and community.

It aims also to improve racial attitudes and behavior now while war morale needs such improvement and "to prepare for the time when our men and women return from the armed services and war industry to peacetime employment."

It is proposed that these enlistees become liaison leaders of age and sex groups in local religious and social agencies to link them into some central interracial committee or commission. Suggestions are made for mutual planning and for counseling with leaders of labor unions and employer organizations, with the Mayor, police officers and other public officials about policies and plans to change unfair economic and social conditions and to be prepared for emergencies when tension arises and conflict threatens.

Leaders in a score of cities are acting on these ideas. Information and experience of the past are being made available in printed form for the instruction and guidance of local leaders. As in all matters of peace, law and order, the good will and sense of fair play of the large majority have to be organized and focused to overcome the ill-will and lawlessness of the selfish and prejudiced.

GEORGE EDMUND HAYNES, RACE RELATIONS SECRETARY, FEDERAL COUNCIL OF CHURCHES, NEW YORK.

Housing Plan Sets Tenancy Standards

BY THE NEW YORK TIMES | DEC. 2, 1945

CHICAGO, DEC. 1 — The American Council on Race Relations has issued in pamphlet form a proposal for a new type of residential property agreement based on occupancy standards, as a substitute for racially restrictive covenants.

"If instead of restrictions on account of race, creed and color," the council said, "there were agreements binding property owners not to sell or lease except to single families, barring excessive roomers and otherwise dealing with the type of occupancy, properties would be better protected during both white and Negro occupancy.

"This would both protect the integrity of the neighborhood and afford an opportunity for the member of a minority group who has the means and the urge to live in a desirable neighborhood.

"It would also prevent, or at least lessen, the exodus of all whites upon the entrance of a few Negroes, and this is what depresses property values."

The plan would permit "selective infiltration of minorities" the council maintained, and would reduce pressure on neighborhoods economically ill adapted for it.

Big Negro Colonies Worry West-Coast

BY GEORGE STREATOR | MAY 4, 1947

SAN FRANCISCO, MAY 3 — The wartime migration of more than 75,000 Negroes into this city and the East Bay area, with the prospect of many more, has posed here, as elsewhere, the problem of housing and unemployment, many leaders said today.

But the leadership itself is difficult to define, although this city now presents a typical Negro ghetto picture, in terms of the number of clubs, churches, councils and fraternal organizations. In addition, there sprang up during the war a multitude of interracial or inter-cultural groups, some from the "left wing," others from orthodox organizations of church liberals.

There are said to be about 100,000 Negroes in the entire Bay region today, although the census of 1940 revealed only 20,000. The rapid expansion of war industry, particularly the growth of the shipbuilding industry, drew Negro colonies to Oakland, Berkeley, Vallejo and this city.

During the war, various pressure groups arose to contest alleged discrimination in the APL trade unions. Most of the charges were filed against the Boilermakers International, which set up separate auxiliaries for Negroes, who, before a series of California court decisions, could pay their dues but could not vote, nor participate in union affairs.

Considerable rancor was thus engendered on the union question, and the word "integration" found its widest usage among Negroes. They sought to be included in the regular affairs of the labor community, and much pressure was put to bear on the shipbuilding companies to make upgrading on the job certain for Negro and other non-white races.

Besides the orthodox National Association for the Advancement of Colored People, and the latecomer, the Urban League, more than eighty of these civil-rights organizations entered the field, either to influence or advise, if not to form, the "patterns" for Negro participation in community life.

Today the picture is blending with the most usual patterns of Negro life. In spite of the efforts made out here to chart a different course, all local Negro settlements are the same as the originals in New York, Chicago or St. Louis.

Dr. William McKinley Thomas who moved to this city in 1945 after service with the Army Medical Corps, was appointed last year, to the local housing authority. A graduate of Meharry Medical College in Nashville, Tenn., he completed his work in Kansas City, Mo.

Dr. Thomas is critical of the leftists, and accuses them of using the Negro out here to further ends that are inimical to the race's welfare. He is opposed to "jim crow" housing, and will try to change the local policy of segregation in permanent public housing.

The American Council on Race Relations, with headquarters in Chicago, and financed by the Rosenwald Fund and Marshall Field, has announced it will suspend activities out here. The director, Laurence I. Hewes sailed for Japan to enter Federal employ. The Negro associate, Matt Crawford, is now employed by the National Negro Congress.

Seaton W. Manning, director of the local Urban League, reported growing unemployment, and said that half the Negro unemployment is found among veterans.

Texas Fights Bias to Insure Supply of Mexican Labor

BY JOHN E. KING | JUL. 4, 1948

DALLAS, TEX., JULY 3 — Whether or not Texas will have enough cotton pickers next fall to harvest its 1948 cotton crop depends largely upon unusual negotiations by a group of individuals with Mexico.

The Mexican Government invoked a powerful economic weapon against the state last October on the grounds of discrimination against Mexican workers. The Mexican alien-labor agreement under which Mexicans were allowed to enter Texas to work was revoked, cutting off the principal supply of transient labor for the cotton harvest.

Mexico charged that Mexicans in Texas faced educational, social and economic discrimination. In some parts of the state Mexican labor was paid for its work at a lower wage than other workers.

SEGREGATION PRACTICED

In thirty-eight school districts in Texas, Mexican students were segregated from other students until they were of junior high school age. Restaurants, theaters, business houses and other public places in many communities barred Mexicans.

To combat this treatment, Mexico refused to allow its workers to enter Texas, and cut off a labor source that in past years has supplied 40,000 to 50,000 cotton pickers.

Without Mexican labor, harvesting of the cotton crop would be nearly impossible, so the Texas Cotton Ginners Association took on the problem. Through its executive secretary, Jay C. Stilley, the association got in touch with the Mexican Government and sought a new agreement. At present it appears that Mexico will allow at least 10,000 workers to come into Texas in the fall.

A tentative agreement is based on the ginners' proposal, known as the Stilley Plan. The ginners have agreed to work with a list prepared by Mexico's Counsul General which shows schools, industrial and agricultural centers where discrimination has been practiced. The ginners are sponsoring meetings to explain to farmers, business men, peace officers and others that for the well-being of the community discriminatory practices against Mexicans must cease.

Local groups will set up boards or committees to investigate discrimination and to work with the ginners association, the Texas Good Neighbor Commission and the Mexican counsul.

Within the last two weeks Gov. Beauford Jester has stepped into the anti-discrimination program by moving to end school segregation. Ginners across the state have enthusiastically adopted the Stilley Plan and have persuaded business men and farmers to eliminate discriminatory practices.

'Wetback' Patrol to Be Stepped Up; 500 Officers to Augment Unit of 256 on Mexico Border to Halt Alien Influx

BY THE NEW YORK TIMES | JUNE 10, 1954

WASHINGTON, JUNE 9 — The Department of Justice announced today that a large round-up of "wetbacks" would begin June 17 along the Mexican border.

Nearly 500 patrolmen from other districts will reinforce the 256-member regular border patrol. Selected areas will be combed for all alien laborers illegally in this country and those apprehended will be deported to Mexico.

"Wetbacks" is a term applied to migrant laborers who sneak across the border from Mexico, often by swimming or wading the Rio Grande. Attorney General Herbert Brownell Jr. said that the apprehensions of "wetbacks" at present were averaging 75,000 a month and the illegal infiltration "has been steadily increasing."

Mr. Brownell announced that he would ask Congress to pass two laws to provide the Justice Department with "much needed weapons" to stamp out "the increasing illegal crossings." These laws would:

1. Authorize a court injunction to restrain an employer from continuing to hire aliens illegally in this country when the employer had knowledge that the alien was an illegal entrant.

2. Authorize seizure and forfeiture of any vehicle or vessel used to transport aliens in violation of the immigration laws.

Mr. Brownell said that the "principal target" of the second law "is the flourishing business of transporting aliens who migrate to this country illegally from Mexico in search of employment."

Mr. Brownell said that the round-up would be concentrated in California and Arizona. It will be under the direction of Joseph M. Swing, Commissioner of the Immigration and Naturalization Service.

CHAPTER 3

The Civil Rights Era

The push for equality incited the protests of the 1950s and 1960s. Rosa Parks instigated the bus boycott in Montgomery, Ala. Brave students overcame efforts to prevent school desegregation in Little Rock, Ark. Malcolm X preached the values of separatism, and Dr. Martin Luther King Jr. inspired 250,000 people into action with his "I Have a Dream" speech in the historic March on Washington.

Racial Issues Stirred by Mississippi Killing

BY JOHN N. POPHAM | SEPT. 18, 1955

An all-white jury deliberated for half an hour before deciding to acquit the two men accused of kidnapping and murdering 14-year-old Emmett Till. The men later publicly admitted to having killed Till. Till's murder and the acquittal of his killers was one of the catalysts that ignited the next period of civil rights activism.

SUMNER, MISS., SEPT. 17 — While hand-laborers and modern mechanized equipment move across the snow-white fields of Mississippi under the hot September sun, a sordid murder case has focused the glare of national attention on the intricate system of race relations which the dominant white group enforces in the name of stability.

In the three-story, gray-brick courthouse of this county seat of Tallahatchie County, the details of the murder case will be dramatized in formal trial proceedings that begin on Monday. But in several senses the real drama will concern the entire state and its role as a militant defender of racial segregation practices.

On Aug. 31, the body of 14-year-old Emmett Till, a Chicago Negro boy, was found in the Tallahatchie River. There was a bullet hole over the right ear, the other side of the head had been bludgeoned and the body was wired to a heavy metal fan that is used in the operating machinery of a cotton gin.

Within forty-eight hours, law enforcement officers of Tallahatchie County and neighboring Leflore County had brought about the arrest of Roy Bryant, 24 years old, and his half-brother, J. W. Milam, 36 years old, on charges of kidnapping young Till. On Sept. 6, an all-white Tallahatchie County Grand Jury indicted both men on murder and kidnapping charges in the death of the Chicago youth.

The story told by the law enforcement officers was that Till had been visiting his 64-year-old uncle, Mose Wright, a cotton field worker of Leflore County. In recent years a great many Negroes have migrated from this section to Chicago to get industrial jobs and during summer months and on holidays there is considerable visiting among the parted family members.

WENT TO THE STORE

On Aug. 24, Till and several other Negro boys went to the grocery store operated by Bryant and his 21-year-old wife at Money, a cotton workers' community of about 200 people in Leflore County hard by the Tallahatchie County line. They were said to have purchased some bubblegum from Mrs. Bryant while she was alone in the store at about 7 P. M.

The Bryant store has been pictured in some reports as a crossroads emporium in a lonely country area. Actually, the store centers in a cluster of buildings, including homes, a cotton-ginning establishment about 100 yards in one direction and a gasoline filling station about twenty-five feet in the opposite direction.

Till reportedly made "some remarks" to Mrs. Bryant in the store and later greeted her with a "wolf whistle" as she walked out of the door to go to her car. It was reported that Till's companions hustled the Chicagoan into their auto and drove away.

On Aug. 28, Till was taken from his uncle's home in the predawn hours by two men. Sheriff George Smith of Leflore County has said that Bryant and Milam told him they took the boy away in their car and that they released him the same day when they became "convinced" he was not the "same boy" who had whistled at Mrs. Bryant.

PUBLIC REACTION

The finding of Till's body and the piecemeal reports of the alleged motivations of the crime touched off an explosion of public reaction in Mississippi, where the subject of race relations has had an inflammatory status by reason of the Supreme Court's historic decision on May 17, 1954, that public school racial segregation laws are unconstitutional.

The reaction to Till's murder reveals the wrenched feelings of Mississippi. The picture is one of white supremacy that skates the thin ice separating it from white tyranny.

Overridingly, the white community of Mississippi reacted to Till's slaying with sincere and vehement expressions of outrage. From one end of the state to the other, newspaper editorials denounced the killing, demanded swift retributive justice and warned that Mississippians could defend their theories of separation of the races only if the law enforcement machinery was geared to equal justice for both races.

Public officials from the Governor down called for determined prosecution in the Till case.

Governor Hugh White and Attorney General J. P. Coleman, who last month won the Democratic gubernatorial nomination which assures him of becoming the next chief executive, moved jointly in naming a special prosecutor to handle the trial of the Till case.

In this instance, perhaps to a depth hitherto unknown in Mississippi race-relations annals, Negroes working in white homes and in downtown stores and restaurants heard on every side a strong and vigorous condemnation by white people, friend and stranger alike, of brutality in race relations. Many of the state's Negro leaders paid tribute to this development.

But the Till killing involves more than a murder case in Mississippi. The reaction to it involves the whole picture of race relations.

In the course of waging an all-out fight to preserve the dual race system in the face of court litigation that has resulted in rulings adverse to Mississippi's views, the state's white leadership has often singled out those it regards as "enemies" and has denounced them in strong language.

Mainly, these "enemies" have been the National Association for the Advancement of Colored People, which has provided legal services for most of the court actions brought by Negroes seeking to expand their civil rights guarantees.

ANGRY OPINION

For many months now public speakers and writers of letters-to-the-editor have blanketed the state with assertions that the N.A.A.C.P. is a "Communist led" organization that seeks to "mongrelize" the races and that the Supreme Court is composed of "political shysters" with a predilection for Communist ideology.

As a consequence of the constantly raging debates over the actions of the N.A.A.C.P., the decisions of the Supreme Court and the impact of all this on the political realm which involves public-office holders at election time, the race relations climate in Mississippi has been extraordinarily touchy.

Therefore it came as no great surprise when the high tide of denunciation of the Till slaying was met with a backwash of opposite reaction in some quarters because of developments that involved the N.A.A.C.P. and "outsiders" in general.

All over the state there were expressions of resentment in which the spectre of the N.A.A.C.P. was exhumed, references were made to "Communist interest" in the Till slaying and the cry of "enemy" was sounded far and wide.

Specifically, the N.A.A.C.P. opponents were angered at having the Till slaying labeled a "lynching," at the demand of public officials in

Illinois for Federal Government action in the case and at reports that Till's body was put on public view in Chicago while donations were solicited for the work of the N.A.A.C.P.

INDIGNATION WANES

To many observers, this counter-reaction in the Till case served to reduce in some measure the indignation that first greeted the disclosure of the killing. More accurately, perhaps, those who were most vehement in their denunciation of the killing continued to hold such sentiments, but their secondary following seemed to fall away.

However, there are those who hope that whatever takes place in Sumner's courtroom, the swift sense of outrage that marked the state's first reaction to the killing will be a lasting item in the race-relations struggles ahead over the public school matter. But at this stage that is only a hope.

Negroes' Boycott Cripples Bus Line

BY THE NEW YORK TIMES | JAN. 8, 1956

MONTGOMERY, ALA., JAN. 7 — The boycott of Montgomery bus lines by Negro riders entered its second month this week with no conciliation in sight.

As a result of the bus company's loss of revenue in the boycott, the City Commission Wednesday raised fares 50 per cent: adult fares from 10 to 15 cents, school fares from 5 to 8 cents. The commission also authorized a 5 cent charge for transfers, which have heretofore been free.

Asking for the increase, the bus company cited losses averaging 22 cents a mile since the boycott began Dec. 5. The losses would run even higher, company spokesmen said, except for a curtailment in service that has reduced mileage by 31 per cent.

Shortly after the boycott began, virtually all service to Negro communities was abolished. Two routes, serving predominantly Negro areas, were abandoned entirely and other routes revised so as to exclude Negro neighborhoods along them.

NEGRO WOMAN CONVICTED

The boycott began with the arrest and conviction of Mrs. Rosa Parks, a Negro seamstress employed by a downtown department store. Mrs. Parks had refused to give up her seat when told to do so by the bus driver.

At the time the incident occured, there were twenty-six Negroes and ten white persons seated in the thirty-six-passenger bus. Law requires the bus driver to segregate the passengers but leaves it within his discretion where the line is to be drawn. Thus, on many routes serving populous Negro areas it is not uncommon to see Negroes occupying all but a few seats.

When the driver asked Mrs. Parks and three other Negroes to give up their seats, a number of white persons were about to board. There were already some white persons standing as well as a number of Negroes. The driver explained later in court that he was "equalizing" seating facilities.

Mrs. Parks refused to yield her seat and was arrested for violation of a city segregation ordinance. Later the charge was changed to read a violation of a state law, which gives bus drivers the power to assign and reassign seating. The law makes it a misdemeanor for anyone to disobey the driver's orders.

Mrs. Parks was found guilty in City Recorder's Court and fined $10. Her attorneys filed notice of appeal. At a mass meeting in a local Negro church the night following the court hearing, Negro citizens were urged not to ride the buses. The following morning Negro patronage was down by an estimated 90 per cent. Today it is close to 100 per cent off.

CONDITIONS LAID DOWN

Negro citizens, led by virtually all the city's Negro ministers, have demanded that three conditions be met before they resume riding the buses. These are:

• Adoption of a "first-come-first-served" rule as is in effect in other Alabama cities such as Mobile and Huntsville. Under this plan Negroes would continue to load from the rear and whites from the front, but the seating, once established, would remain fixed.

• Greater courtesy on the part of drivers. Negro bus riders have complained of rude, insulting treatment.

• Employment of Negro drivers on routes serving predominently Negro areas.

A bi-racial committee, appointed by the City Commission, has so far failed to resolve any of the differences. The company contends that it cannot adopt a "first-come-first-served" policy and comply with the segregation laws. Negotiations have been broken off, for the time at least.

Militia Sent to Little Rock; School Integration Put Off

BY BENJAMIN FINE | **SEPT. 3, 1957**

LITTLE ROCK, ARK., TUESDAY, SEPT. 3 — Gov. Orval E. Faubus sent militia-men and state police last night to Little Rock High School, where racial integration had been scheduled to start today.

The Governor, a foe of integration, said troops were necessary to prevent violence and bloodshed at the school.

By early morning about 100 members of the state militia had sur-rounded the school. They were armed with billy clubs, rifles and bayo-nets. Some carried gas masks.

The Board of Education met with Dr. Virgil Blossom, Superinten-dent of Schools, late last evening to consider the new developments. It then issued a statement appealing to Negroes not to attempt to pass through the line of troops. The board's statement said:

"Although the Federal Court has ordered integration to proceed, Governor Faubus has said schools should continue as they have in the past and has stationed troops at Central High School to main-tain order.

"In view of the situation, we ask that no Negro students attempt to attend Central or any other white high school until this dilemma is legally resolved."

The Federal District Court last Friday upheld a previous court order that integration should begin today. Judge Ronald N. Davies, in a special hearing Friday afternoon, enjoined any and all persons from interfering with the integration program. Judge Davies acted after a county judge, Murray O. Reed, had issued an injunction against integration.

School officials did not know what the next legal move would be.

Twelve Negroes had been scheduled to attend the high school this morning.

The militia at the school is under the direction of Maj. Gen, Sherman T. Clinger. General Clinger would not say whether he would keep out any Negro students who might attempt to enter,

"We will do everything necessary," he said, "to preserve the peace. That is our mission as given to us by the Governor."

In his television talk last night. Governor Faubus said he was calling out the militia because he had heard that violence would break out when schools opened.

He said that many persons in Little Rock had purchased knives and other weapons. He also said that a number of revolvers had. been taken from high school students, both white and Negro.

"I have reports of caravans that will converge upon Little Rock from many parts of the state and members of the caravans are to assemble peaceably upon the school grounds in the morning. Some of these groups have already reached the city."

The Governor also said that there was a telephone campaign going on in the city calling on the mothers of white children to assemble on the school grounds at 6 o'clock this morning. Because of these threats of disorder, violence and possible bloodshed, he said, he has called out the National Guard. However, he said that even with the Guardsmen present, keeping the peace might be difficult.

"I must state here in all sincerity, that it is my opinion, yes, even a conviction, that it will not be possible to restore or to maintain order and protect the lives and property of the citizens if forceable integration is carried out tomorrow in the schools of this community," the Governor said.

"The inevitable conclusion, therefore, must be that the schools in Pulaski County, for the time being, must be operated on the same basis as they have been operated in the past."

"This is a decision," Governor Faubus said, "that I have reached prayerfully, after conferences with dozens of people. The mission of the state militia is to maintain order. They will not act as segregationists or integrationists but as soldiers."

He said that even with the militia it might not be possible to maintain order if "forceful integration is carried out to-morrow."

Governor Faubus said:

"The inevitable conclusion is that the schools must be operated as they have in the past. I appeal to the reason of all. Let us all be good citizens. The public peace will be preserved."

"This is a situation not of my making," he said. "The plan for integration has been set up by the Little Rock school board and the superintendent. The majority of the people of this community are opposed to integration."

Under the plan integration will take place on a gradual basis. This fall the senior high schools will have mixed classes. In 1960, if all goes smoothly, Negroes will be admitted to the junior high school. By 1963 the elementary grades will be thrown open to all students, regardless of color.

Thus, in six years, under the plan, the entire school system will be integrated.

Extremists on both sides are unhappy.

The National Association for the Advancement of Colored People has declared six years to be too long a period. It brought a Federal suit to hasten integration, but the judges ruled that the School Board had shown good faith and was proceeding with all deliberate speed.

The White Citizens Councils and other anti-integrationist groups oppose any degree of integration now or at any fore-seeable time.

Amis Guthridge, attorney for the Capital Citizens Council, a local of the Arkansas White Citizens Councils, said today that "we will continue to fight in a peaceful manner to maintain the high principles upon which our Southern society was founded."

It was at seemingly the eleventh hour that Governor Faubus jumped into the fight to prevent integration. He appeared last week at a State Chancery Court hearing on an injunction petition brought in the name of the League of Central High Mothers.

He told the court that there would be rioting and bloodshed if the city program was put into effect and that the Federal Government would not intervene. He urged that the school board be enjoined from going ahead with its plans. An injunction was granted by Chancellor Murray O. Reed of the court.

Granting of the injunction was immediately challenged by the school officials. They cited that they were under orders from the Federal District Court to integrate without delay. The issue was resolved Friday afternoon when Federal Judge Ronald N. Davies overruled the state decision.

In its planning the board of education has taken into consideration the possibility of violence, Dr. Blossom has met with police officials and with other community leaders on steps to avoid conflict.

Negro Protests Lead to Store Closings

BY THE NEW YORK TIMES | FEB. 7, 1960

GREENSBORO, N. C., FEB. 6 — The P. W. Woolworth Company and S. H. Kress & Company closed their stores here this afternoon. Negroes who had been seeking service at the lunch counters hailed the move as a victory.

The Woolworth management said a telephone call had been received at 1:15 P. M. saying a bomb had been placed in the basement. The store was then closed.

The Negro students, from North Carolina Agricultural and Technical College, Bennett College and Dudley High School, moved to the Kress store and sat at the stools. Kress then closed.

The protest by the Negroes began Monday. Each day since then the students have sat at the counters even though they have been refused service. By the middle of the week a number of white men and boys were vying with the Negroes for seats.

Negro Rejected at Mississippi U.; U. S. Seeks Writs

BY CLAUDE SITTON | SEPT. 21, 1962

OXFORD, MISS., SEPT. 20 — Gov. Ross R. Barnett denied James H. Meredith, a 29-year-old Negro, admission to the University of Mississippi today. In so doing, the Governor defied orders of the Federal courts. The Justice Department took steps immediately to obtain contempt of court citations against Dr. J. D. Williams, university chancellor; Dr Robert B. Ellis, the registrar and Dean Arthur B. Lewis.

All three were named in Federal court desegregation orders directing the admission of Mr. Meredith to the all-white institution.

[In Meridian, Miss., according to The Associated Press, Federal District Judge Sidney C. Mize ordered the three university officials to appear before him Friday and show cause why they should not be cited for contempt. He acted at the request of Justice Department lawyers.]

CRITICAL CONFLICT

In rejecting the application of Mr. Meredith, an Air Force veteran, Mr. Barnett set the stage for one of the most critical conflicts between state and Federal authority yet seen in the South. The controversy poses grave problems of international significance for the Kennedy Administration.

Shortly before flying here from Jackson, the state capital, Governor Barnett persuaded the Board of Trustees of Institutions of Higher Learning to appoint him as special registrar to deal with the "registration or non-registration" of the Negro student.

The Governor, his aides and their supporters had waged a behind-the-scenes campaign for almost a week to force the trustees to invest him with this authority.

One trustee, Tally Riddell of Quitman, suffered a heart seizure late last night as the board conferred in a conference room at the University of Mississippi Medical Center in Jackson. His condition was reported to be not serious.

Governor Barnett, who has asserted his willingness to go to jail to prevent the desegregation of the university, confronted Mr. Meredith today in a dramatic, 20-minute meeting. It took place behind the curtained glass doors of the Mississippi Center for Continuation Studies on the campus.

Approximately 100 uniformed State Highway patrolmen and scores of sheriffs, deputies, plainclothesmen and policemen held back a crowd of 2,000 jeering students.

As the automobile carrying Mr. Meredith and Federal officials pulled away toward Memphis, the students swarmed across a grassy, tree-shaded mall in a futile attempt to stop them.

Mr. Meredith was accompanied by St. John Barrett, second assistant Attorney General in the Civil Rights Division of the Justice Department; James McShane, chief United States marshal, and an unidentified deputy marshal.

STATEMENT IS BRIEF

Following their departure, Governor Barnett emerged and told newsmen: "The only statement I have to make is this: The application of James Meredith was refused."

During the meeting, the Federal officials served Dr. Ellis, the registrar, and Governor Barnett with copies of the injunctions directing Mr. Meredith's admission. They were issued by the Federal District Court and the United States Court of Appeals for the Fifth Circuit.

A law enforcement official who was present said Mr. Ellis had given way to Governor Barnett after reading the court order. Acting as a special registrar, the latter then denied the Negro student's application.

One of the Federal officials asked the Governor if he realized he was in contempt of court along with officials of the university and the trustees, according to the law enforcement officer.

The Governor was said to have replied by asking if the Federal official was telling him or whether this would be done by the court.

Officials found guilty of contempt are subject to heavy civil and criminal penalties and the possibility of a prison term limited only by the prisoner's willingness to purge himself by obeying the court.

There are no immediate indications as to the outcome of the dispute, which comes during the week of the 100th anniversary of the Emancipation Proclamation under which President Lincoln declared slaves in the Confederate States free.

Governor Barnett threw down the gauntlet of defiance in a television address a week ago tonight. He invoked the legally discredited doctrine of interposition. By this act, he contended, he "interposed" the power of the state between, the Federal Government and the university and thus nullified the desegregation order. If the Governor's present strategy fails, his only apparent recourse is to close the university.

Mr. Barnett stepped into the situation today after attorneys for the Justice Department and the N.A.A.C.P. Legal Defense and Educational. Fund had blocked attempts by the Legislature, state courts and officials to halt Mr. Meredith's admission.

Only this morning, Homer Edgeworth, a Justice of the Peace in Jackson, found Mr. Meredith guilty of a charge of falsifying a voter-registration application. The student, who remained at the home of a Negro lawyer in Memphis until he was driven here, was not present for the proceedings. Mr. Edgeworth sentenced the student to a year in jail and fined him $500.

Justice Department attorneys went before Federal District Judge Harold Cox and Sidney Mize at Meridian, Miss., and obtained an order striking down the conviction.

It was a clear, sparkling day in the high seventies here in Oxford, the home of the late William Faulkner. The novelist lies buried on a hill across town from the oak-shaded university campus.

Students gathered early this morning on the grassy mall in front of the Lyceum Building, where the Negro student was expected to pick up registration and fee cards.

At one point more than 500 students swarmed rowdily to the center of the mall and pulled the American flag halfway down its pole before student leaders stopped them.

Two coeds danced the twist with two youths on the asphalt drive before the lyceum. Students responded to this performance with boos and cries of "Mickey Mouse."

Governor Barnett landed at the nearby Oxford Airport at 2:45 P.M. accompanied by Lieut. Gov. Paul B. Johnson. They were flown up from Jackson in a highway patrol plane.

Both officials went immediately to the Study Center, a one-story modernistic building of red brick on the edge of the campus.

Exactly at 4 P.M. a caravan of highway patrol cruisers began rolling across the railroad bridge that separates town and campus. Seventy-five husky troopers in Confederate gray and armed with revolvers cleared the lawn in front of the center and took up positions along the drive.

Students began to stream across the park in front of the building from the Lyceum Building and several climbed trees to get a better view.

The Meredith party, riding in a green and white sedan escorted by an automobile driven by deputy United States Marshals pulled up at 4:30 P.M. A chorus of boos went up and one student shouted: "Go home, nigger."

Mr. Meredith, dressed in a brown suit and white shirt, got out of the car and looked for a moment at the crowd. Then turning, with a furrowed brow, he walked with his escort into the building.

There was little tension among the students, who apparently believed that this was only an assault — not a breach — in the university's racial barrier. Fifteen minutes later, the crowd set up a football chant: "Hoddy toddy, gosh almighty, who in the hell are we. Hey, eh, flim flam, bim bam, Ole Miss by damn."

This was followed by yells of "we want Ross!"

Federal officials, led by Mr. Barnett, walked out of the doorway at 4:51 P.M. Mr. Meredith followed them with a tight-lipped smile on his face. They got into the car and drove away.

Violence in Mississippi Has Roots in Slavery Furor of the 1830's; Racial Views Are Probably Unshaken

BY CLAUDE SITTON | OCT. 3, 1962

OXFORD, MISS., OCT. 2 — Small, white rectangles of paper lay trampled amid the broken glass and brickbats on the tree-shaded oval in front of the University of Mississippi administration building. The slogan "Ross is Right' was stamped in bold, red letters across their face.

The cards had served to identify the hard core of the mob that carried defiance of Federal authority to the ultimate on Sunday night, leaving death and destruction in its wake.

They also offered symbolic tribute to Gov. Ross R. Barnett, who swore resistance to the bitter end against the Federal court orders that brought desegregation to Ole Miss.

MANY REGRET ACTS

Many Mississippians regret the violent acts of those who pinned the cards over their hearts and laid siege to a force of 300 deputy United States marshals. But it seems doubtful that the regret has shaken their belief in the slogan under which the mob fought.

The views on states rights and segregation expressed by the Governor as he charted his course of defiance appear to constitute the orthodox doctrine adhered to by a majority of whites.

For many of them, defense of this doctrine has taken on the aura of a holy crusade. For others it has become the means to an end.

Students of the state's history trace the roots of this orthodoxy to the heritage of slavery and the relative poverty and ignorance from which Mississippi is now struggling to escape They say these beliefs have been perpetuated by an establishment consisting of the "Four P's," politicians, preachers, press and philosophers.

A PROFESSOR'S VIEW

Mississippi, according to a professor at the university took its leave from the main stream of American thought in 1830 and has never returned. This resulted from the attack on slavery by Northern abolitionists.

Within 20 years, an "orthodox view" had been established. Opposition was squelched and those who refused to conform or acquiesce left the state. Sources of information on the thinking of the rest of the nation were shut off, the professor said.

The state's leaders, in the professor's words, ceased to react to public issues in terms of established fact but were governed instead by the orthodox view. "They stopped thinking," he said.

The Civil War's aftermath of poverty and bitterness demanded an explanation. "Looking back, they couldn't blame the war because they brought it on," the professor said. "So they blamed it on reconstruction and glorified the war."

White supremacists who took over the state's political leadership before the turn of the century found support for segregation in the pro-slavery argument of an earlier day.

Some of those arguments are still being employed by Governor Barnett, who is considered a political descendant of such advocates of white supremacy as the late Senator Theodore Bilbo.

Despite this heritage, Mississippians recall the Supreme Court's public school desegregation decision in 1954 was received with relative calm.

'RELUCTANT ACQUIESCENCE'

The Rev. Duncan M. Gray, rector of St. Peter's Episcopal Church here, said there was a feeling of "reluctant acquiescence" in many parts of the state. He said a county school superintendent in the Delta had remarked at the time, "What else can you expect in a Christian and democratic country."

A short time later, however, Senator James O. Eastland, a political power in the state, began asserting that the decision was not the law of the land and therefore did not have to be obeyed.

The first chapter of the militantly segregationist Citizens Councils was founded at Indianola, near the Senator's home. The councils soon spread to other areas of the state.

Mr. Gray contends that there was a lack of national leadership on the issue under President Eisenhower and that this discouraged advocates of compliance with the court decrees.

CONFORMITY ENFORCED

The segregationists moved into the asserted vacuum. The power of the political establishment, largely made up of conservative planters and businessmen, enforced conformity. And the Citizens Councils set out on a campaign to purge or silence their opponents.

The frightened and the expedient hastened to "get right of segregation," while the cynical moved to take political advantage of the additional vote promised by the issue.

The philosophers referred to by the university professor began to emerge. One of the first was Judge Tom Brady, who excoriated the Supreme Court decision in his book, "Black Monday."

The statements of South Carolina's John C. Calhoun on the power of the states to nullify those acts of the Federal Government that they found objectionable were combed for ammunition.

A latecomer to the ranks was Carleton Putnam, an airline director and Northerner, whose book, "Race and Reason," purports to prove the inherent inferiority of the Negro race.

LEGALITY DENIED

Lawyers attacked the desegregation decision on legal grounds.

Many ministers cited Biblical passages to prove their contention that segregation is the will of God. Others remained silent on the issue and only a few spoke out for obedience to the courts.

The larger newspapers and the radio and television stations in the Jackson area gave wholehearted support to the Citizens Councils and to the prosegregation campaign of propaganda.

Other newspapers with wide circulation opposed desegregation and gave little more than lip service to the principle of law and order where the racial issue was involved. They also aided the councils indirectly by praising questionable anti-Communist programs while the councils attacked desegregation as a "Red Plot."

The State Sovereignty Commission voted tax funds to help the councils finance their program in Mississippi and other states.

The climate of opinion in Mississippi at the time of Governor Barnett's thrice-repeated refusal to honor the orders of the courts was reflected in the comments of Judge M. M. McGowan as written for The Clarion-Ledger and Jackson Daily News of last Sunday.

"The courageous stand of Governor Barnett for the rights of the states and for liberty and freedom of the people has electrified the South, and in fact the entire nation," he wrote.

"There are two features of this momentous event that stand out with clarity. First, the looming up of a strong leader, who, it seemed for so long, would never make his appearance, and around whom the people of the South and of the entire nation could rally; the second, the accelerated breaking up of the almost glacial complacency of the people."

'DEADLY ENCROACHMENT'

Judge McGowan continued: "We witness the deadly encroachment of socialism; the image of actual Communism showing its ugly head in our own government; reckless and power-drunk bureaucrats illegally seeking dictatorial powers; judicial tyranny; vicious assaults upon the businessmen who built our nation and pay its revenues; the conspiracy to bankrupt and destroy our nation by giving its substance to our enemies; law by injunction and an endless train of other abuses cruelly designed to stamp out the last vestiges of our constitutional rights."

Viewed against this background, the taunts shouted at Federal troops by University of Mississippi students were not surprising to observers.

"Yankees, go home," they jeered. "Why don't you go to Cuba?"

Nor were these observers surprised when some of the students compared their opposition to desegregation with the resistance of the Hungarian freedom fighters.

"The leaders of Mississippi have deceived the people not only in terms of these spurious intellectual arguments but also by telling them that they did not have to obey the Federal courts," Mr. Gray said.

The clergyman noted that many of the younger students present at the riot scene had been only 10 years old at the time of the Supreme Court's decision. He said they had been steeped in the propaganda of defiance.

"Governor Barnett has become the symbol of lawlessness," he asserted. "If the Governor can defy the courts, why can't a freshman at Ole Miss?"

The Commercial Appeal of Memphis put it in even stronger terms in an editorial today. "Worst of all was the political demagoguery which led the elected leaders of Mississippi to stand back and pretend that because the Federal marshal brought Meredith to Ole Miss the state was no longer compelled to uphold the peace," the newspaper said.

"The Governor calls this an invasion, although Mississippi National Guardsmen are participating in the Federal action. He has used the Mississippi Highway Patrol to keep Meredith out of Ole Miss, while he could, but has permitted it to step back when civil strife tore his state apart.

"While the caravans of agitators poured onto the campus, Mr. Barnett said nothing. Not a Mississippi official rose to reprimand them."

DENY INTEGRATION OCCURRED

Although the Governor lost his battle to prevent the admission of James H. Meredith to the university, the segregationist forces display no readiness to concede the war. Mr. Barnett has contended publicly that the 29-year-old Negro's admission did not constitute integration. And the Governor and his supporters have placed blame for the riot on the deputy United States marshals.

The establishment, temporarily shaken by the two deaths, numerous injuries and the property destruction left by the mob, already appears to be closing ranks behind the Governor.

Senator Eastland has called for a Congressional investigation of the marshals' behavior.

"Of course, the unfortunate firing of the gas shells provoked by the students and others, which apparently detonated the activities which followed," he said in a statement.

The television cameraman and his wife who were attacked by students, the marshal who was struck by a length of pipe and the soldiers who were chased from the cabs of their trucks — all before the tear gas was released — would likely disagree.

The Jackson Daily News offered the segregationist explanation of events at the university.

"Until the invasion from outside by both Federals and the civilians not a single case of untoward conduct was to be found," The News said in an editorial.

"The ugly incident shows what racial agitators will go to achieve a propaganda goal to embarrass a decent, law-abiding people, patriotic Americans who have the intelligence to detect their diabolical designs."

The News also offered a portent of the future. "When it comes to supporting those customs and traditions which produced a tranquil society for us all, that fight has just begun," the newspaper said.

A sorority house mother at Ole Miss, concerned because some of her charges were attempting to transfer to other schools, said she hoped the relative calm at the university would lead them to change their minds.

"I believe it's leveling off," she said. "I think we will get rid of the nigger. That's the only way it will be settled."

Negro Planning Jobless March

BY THE NEW YORK TIMES | FEB. 25, 1963

BAL HARBOUR, FLA., FEB. 24 — A. Philip Randolph is planning a mass Negro "pilgrimage" to Washington to dramatize what he calls the "unemployment crisis" among Negroes.

Mr. Randolph is the nation's top union Negro leader. He said he would call a meeting of the executive board of the Negro-American Labor Council next month to map plans for the pilgrimage. He said that Negro union leaders also would seek a meeting with President Kennedy to discuss the unemployment situation.

Mr. Randolph heads the Negro Labor Council, formed several years ago to fight within unions against racial barriers to employment and promotion. He also is president of the Brotherhood of Sleeping Car Porters and the only Negro on the 29-member executive council of the American Federation of Labor and Congress of Industrial Organizations. The executive council is holding its midwinter meeting here.

DOUBLE THE UNEMPLOYMENT

Unemployment among Negroes runs more than twice as high as among whites. Last month the unemployment rate reported for whites by the Bureau of Labor Statistics was 5.9 per cent and among Negroes, 12.7.

Negroes also suffer disproportionately from long-term unemployment. They make up about 11 per cent of the population, but represent 24 per cent of those who have been unemployed for 15 or more weeks and 26 per cent of those out of work for half a year or more.

Furthermore nearly 28 per cent of all unemployed Negroes have been out of work for 15 or more weeks, while 24 per cent of the unemployed whites are in this group. About 14 per cent of the Negro jobless, as opposed to 11 per cent of the whites, have been looking for work for half a year or more.

A. Philip Randolph in 1963.

Mr. Randolph said this situation would get worse unless forceful measures were taken quickly to remedy it. Automation and other labor-saving devices are rapidly wiping out the unskilled and semi-skilled jobs, which Negroes hold in large numbers.

Although it is hurting Negroes in this respect, rapid technological change is helping them in another, Mr. Randolph said. It is obliterating old craft lines and, by making special skills a prerequisite for many jobs, breaking down the seniority system.

SENIORITY TROUBLES

Outside of overt bars to employment on racial grounds, Negroes regard the seniority system in union contracts as their greatest obstacle to equal employment opportunity. Under such rules, workers are laid off and recalled in order of their length of service. The slogan is, "Last hired, first fired."

Negroes, who often were the last to be hired because of discrimination, find that discrimination is perpetuated by the seniority system, even after it has been eliminated as a bar to getting a job.

Seniority is a basic principle with most unions, but Mr. Randolph has not found his colleagues sympathetic to junking it. He hopes automation may accomplish that.

The last time Mr. Randolph proposed a Negro march on Washington was early in World War II. His purpose was to win for Negroes, jobs in defense industry. President Franklin D. Roosevelt agreed to Mr. Randolph's proposals, and the unionist called off the demonstration. Late in the war Mr. Randolph told President Harry S. Truman that he would urge Negroes not to serve in the armed forces unless they were integrated, and Mr. Truman acted to accomplish that.

The A.F.L.C.I.O. executive council issued statements over the week-end critical of the Kennedy Administration's tax and economic proposals.

"America is headed for another recession this year, if present economic trends are permitted to run their normal course," the council said. "There is nothing in business developments or Administration programs and proposals to provide confidence that substantial improvements are on the way, even in the next few years."

The council said a tax cut of $10,000,000,000 was needed this year. The Administration has proposed a net cut of that amount, but it would not take full effect for three years.

New York's Racial Unrest: Negroes' Anger Mounting

BY LAYHMOND ROBINSON | AUG. 12, 1963

NAILED OVER THE DOOR of the Church of God and True Holiness on Harlem's 135th Street is a freshly painted sign that reads: "Protest Meeting Every Monday — 8:30 P.M."

A Negro lawyer, waving his hand at the sign as he passed it the other day, declared: "See that? See that? That thing expresses my sentiments exactly. Only I would change it to read 'Protest Meeting Every Monday, Tuesday, Wednesday, Thursday, Friday, Saturday, and Sunday.' "

The sign and the lawyer's amendments to it are symbols of a rising discontent in the Negro districts of the metropolitan area. The resentment among the 1,500,000 black residents in the city and its suburbs, long built-up, has found an outlet. Negroes and their supporters have taken to the streets in an assault on racial segregation and discrimination.

In scenes similar to those in Birmingham, Ala.; Jackson, Miss., and other centers of racial strife, sit-ins, kneel-ins, pray-ins, sleep-ins, hunger strikes, boycotts and freedom marches have taken place. Hundreds of praying, chanting demonstrators have been jailed. Scattered violence has broken out. Some say more violence is inevitable.

Suddenly, it seems, the Negro is mad at everybody.

The protest movement has arisen in a region that has more laws to protect the civil rights of Negroes and other citizens than any other place in America. It has shaken many New Yorkers, who view their city and its environs as a racial melting pot — as the historic haven of the disadvantaged immigrant and the oppressed minority.

To shock New Yorkers — both white and black, some of whom have remained apathetic or supported minor separatist movements — is precisely the goal of the wave of mass demonstrations for integration.

"Our aim is to force the people of this city to sit up and take notice of the injustices Negroes have suffered from for a hundred years!" a speaker at a Brooklyn rally shouted the other night.

"The mood of the Negro is one of impatience, anger and insistence," asserts Percy E. Sutton, a Harlem lawyer who has participated in sit-ins, picketing and civil rights rallies.

"He seeks a final breakthrough, a final toppling of the walls of segregation and discrimination. He has learned, much to his sorrow, that he can't get these things by promises — that he's got to go out and get his equality — that it won't come to him."

VICTORIES WHET APPETITE

Each victory in the movement sharpens the appetite of the demonstrators for another battle.

Mrs. Jean Booker was one of those in the picket line that forced the suspension of construction at the Harlem Hospital annex.

"Our people are incensed," she declared. "How long are they supposed to wait to get decent jobs and homes and schools? They've been revolting quietly for some time. Now it's out in the open."

Mrs. Alice Gill, a Queens housewife and former Government worker, insisted that: "Many Negroes have lost faith in the word of the white man. They took to the streets because they were tired of begging and asking."

Walter Petry, a post office employee, put it this way: "I think the fact that this is the hundredth anniversary of the Emancipation Proclamation had a lot to do with the blowup. Many Negroes were shocked to discover that they've been kicked around for a hundred years. A hundred years has a frightening ring to it. they decided they weren't going to wait another hundred."

'SHOWDOWN HAS COME'

"The showdown has come!" an ebony-skinned demonstrator, his arms extended toward the heavens, shouted on a Brooklyn street corner.

"It's now or never. The show-down is here and we're ready for it, Lord. Men, women and children, we're ready for it."

The tide seems to have swept away the Negro moderate in the city's Negro communities. In recent weeks some speakers at civil rights rallies who have urged moderation and caution have been loudly booed.

A survey by The Times shows, however, that a significant portion of the Negro community lives on a plateau of apathy and indifference toward the battle.

The Negroes' impassive faces and indifferent responses to questions testify to the attitude that, for them, New York is a place where the poor, the unskilled and the uneducated face an indefinite future in the slums.

Such a response came from a thin, shirtless man sitting on a stoop on 118th Street: "Man, just lemme alone. I don't care about nothing. It's too hot to bother about all this noise about integration."

MANY UNCONVINCED

But the protest movement is sweeping forward with an emotional force that is drawing an increasing number of the apathetic. Many continue to remain convinced, however, that the movement won't change their condition in any material way.

There is also another segment of the Negro community that is angry over the Negro's treatment at the hands of the white man — and it demands a change. But it insists on segregation — not integration — as the black man's salvation. It is represented most vocally by the Black Muslims, a religious sect, and by various black nationalist and African nationalist organizations, most of them based in Harlem.

The separatist movements are thus far only minor, compared to the integrationist drive, which is carrying along most of the Negro community.

Some of the Negro's militancy on civil rights is spontaneous. Some of it has been fanned by organizations, two of which — the Urban League and the National Association for the Advancement of Colored People — have spearheaded the battle for Negro rights for more than half a century.

The fires of racial friction in the South have helped spark the movement in New York, as have the flames of independence and nationalism

Malcolm X, an outspoken lieutenant of the militant Black Muslims, promoted the group's separatist policies during a civil rights demonstration in New York City on July 1.

in Black Africa. So have the pressures of the cold war between the United States and the Soviet Union.

Pro-integration sentiment is running as strong on the tree-lined streets of the Negro middle-class districts as it is on the hot and crowded streets of Harlem and other slum areas.

This mood is reflected in such statements as one by Representative Adam Clayton Powell Jr., Harlem's preacher-politician: "What do we Negroes want? We want the same thing the white man wants, and we want it right now — this afternoon!"

It is reflected in the statement of Junius Brown, Negro factory worker: "White folks ain't going to give you nothing. You've got to go out and take it. That's what they did."

Other insistent waves of protest have raced through the Negro community since the Civil War era.

HARLEM IS THE HOME

Since Negroes began to move into Harlem in the first decade of this century, the community has been a cauldron of discontent. It has come to be known as the spiritual home of the Negro protest movement.

During World War I, and for several years following, Marcus Garvey's "Back-to-Africa" movement excited a considerable portion of the Negro community.

In 1925, internal bickering and the conviction and imprisonment of Garvey for mail fraud brought the movement crashing down. But then, as now, most Negroes in the city preferred to remain in the United States.

Communist activities drew a good deal of attention in the nineteen-thirties and forties in Harlem. Harlem helped elect a Communist, Benjamin Davis, to the City Council in World War II. But Communism failed to take deep root and has now disappeared from Harlem.

In World War II, Harlem Negroes, led by A. Philip Randolph, the president of the Brotherhood of Sleeping Car Porters, prepared a march on Washington to pressure President Franklin D. Roosevelt into banning racial discrimination in hiring by defense plants. The march was called off when the President issued an executive order banning such discrimination.

BIGGEST IN AREA'S HISTORY

But the current explosion over civil rights is the biggest — and seems sure to become the most sustained — in the history of the metropolitan area. Civil rights groups view it as possibly the last massive assault against "Northern-style" discrimination and segregation in New York.

James Farmer, national director of the Congress of Racial Equality describes "an under-current of racism" in this and other Northern cities. "It must be brought into the open before we can deal with it," he says. The demonstrations, he adds, are spotlighting it and forcing it into the open.

This is one of the ways in which the rights groups have deliberately sought to stimulate the current movement.

"The demonstrations serve as an emotional release, a focal point of participation for the masses," observes Mr. Randolph, who is currently planning another march on Washington on Aug. 28, some 20 years after he planned the first one. He said: "The situation is so crucial than an outlet has to be provided for the common people to liberate themselves, to release pent-up frustrations that could explode into violence. These demonstrations give them this outlet."

What built up the pressures that have to be released by demonstrations? Negroes insist that though the city and its suburban areas are covered by many civil rights laws banning discrimination and segregation in housing, schools, public accommodations and other areas of public life, these laws have never been properly enforced.

They also point to the fact that the Negro slum districts are spreading rather than shrinking. Labor economists of the United States Bureau of the Census note that the Negro male earns only about three-fifths of what the white male earns on the average, and that this gap is growing wider among the unskilled and semi-skilled workers, who are being hit hard by automation.

Herbert Hill, the N.A.A.C.P. labor secretary, points out that unemployment of Negroes consistently is two to three times that of whites, and that joblessness is growing among the unskilled and semi-skilled Negroes.

PRESSURES OF POPULATION

Population pressures add to the general unrest. New York City's Negro population jumped from 61,000 — or less than 2 per cent of its total population in 1900 — to 1,100,000, or about 15 per cent of the city's population in 1963. About 1,500,000 Negroes live in the metropolitan region, most of them jammed into slum districts.

Many Negroes have come to New York, as others have done, thinking that the streets were paved with gold. They found out otherwise.

"We came up here looking for the Promised Land and didn't find it," asserts a Negro truck driver. "If the boss don't discriminate against you the unions do. You live in a hole the landlords call an apartment and your children go to nothing schools."

"Despite some gains, despite all the laws protecting his rights, the Negro has been for generations overcrowded, underemployed, frustrated and poor," declares Edward S. Lewis, executive director of the Urban League of Greater New York.

DANGER FROM DROPOUTS

Social dynamite, he argues, is building up among high school students who are dropping out of school "at an alarming rate, partly because they have no hope of getting a break in life."

About 25,000 to 40,000 children drop out of the New York City public schools each year, according to school officials. Though no racial census is kept, at least half are Negroes.

"All these years Negroes in the North have been getting big promises and making little or no gains in jobs, education and housing," insists Dr. Kenneth B. Clark, City College psychology professor, and a Negro.

"Now suddenly they realize they've been trampled on for a hundred years. In that time there's been as much backtracking on civil rights as there has been progress, and Negroes are fed up."

Dr. Clark, whose testimony on behalf of Negro children played a key role in the Supreme Court's 1954 school integration cases, points to other things that helped light the fuse of the current Negro revolt.

"Events in Birmingham and Jackson — the fire hoses and the police dogs, James Meredith and Ole Miss — all have angered Negroes in the North," the professor contends. "but the terrible unemployment here among Negroes, the bad housing, the bad schools — all contributed to the blowup."

"Our people are trapped," says Moses Brown, a laborer. "All they know is they got to get out of this trap somehow. They got to fight for it."

Civil rights laws, numerous as they are, have never been vigorously enforced by the city or the state, argues J. Raymond Jones, Harlem City Councilman.

Moreover, he says, some labor unions practicing discrimination have been virtually immune from the state and city laws on antidiscrimination because of their political power. This has been especially true, he asserts, of the "aristocrats of the union movement — the craft unions."

On this point he would find wide agreement in the Negro community. Much of the current protest has been directed at unions in the building trades and other crafts.

"No white man's going to tell me when I'm ready for my rights," says Philip B. Robinson, an unemployed metal worker. "I'm ready for my rights now and I'm going to get them one way or another."

Mr. Randolph points out that many skilled Negro workers drift into menial jobs after they migrate from the South because they cannot join the craft unions and thus have difficulty practicing their trades.

Another important target of the demonstrators — and of court suits — has been the public school systems in the city and suburbs.

With the aid of lawyers for the N.A.A.C.P. and individual lawyers a multiplicity of suits has been filed by parents challenging "de facto" segregation in the schools.

These parents have charged that the schools are inferior because of poor teaching, poor equipment, old buildings and other items. Picketing and boycotts have been commonplace, and a general Negro boycott of the schools has been threatened by Negro parent groups.

HOUSING DISCRIMINATION

Strong resentment has also built up over housing discrimination and slum conditions, though the city and the state have the strongest laws in the country forbidding discrimination in both public and private housing. Moreover, many "housekeeping" laws are regulations aimed at preventing the growth of slum conditions in multiple dwellings.

Here again, Negro civil rights officials, as well as Negroes on the street, say that a lot of lip service has been given to these laws, but that there has been a little actual enforcement.

Hulan E. Jack, former Manhattan Borough President, warns of a "blowup" over housing conditions in the 14th Assembly District in Harlem, where he serves as Democratic district leader. "You can feel the tension over these stinking housing conditions rising up like heat from the sidewalks," he remarked on a sultry night recently as he walked along 116th Street near Lenox Avenue.

"Rats are taking over some of these buildings," he exclaimed, waving his arms at the rows of tenements. "And you think people should accept this — that their children should have to live in this? Why, some people around here are ready to kill landlords.

COLD WAR IMPACT FELT

But unemployment, poor housing and poor schools are not the only causes of the civil rights revolt in the metropolitan area.

The rise of the black nations of Africa and the pressures of the cold war have had a heavy impact on it, some observers contend.

"Negroes here see other black people who were subjugated only a few years ago presiding over their countries as prime ministers, presidents and ambassadors," City Councilman Jones comments. "Then they turn around and ask why they haven't made more progress in what is supposed to be the most democratic and advanced country in the world."

Others close to the Negro community hold that United States competition with the Soviet Union has forced the Federal Government and state and city governments to take a more active role in championing the rights of minorities since World War II.

"It's put-up or shut-up time," one civil rights official says. "People in this country have got to come across or stop yakking about equality and freedom for the rest of the world."

"The Negro has got to take advantage of this atmosphere," another observed. "He's got to strike while the iron is hot. The final breakthrough to complete, final and lasting equality must be won now — or the change may never come again."

APATHY REMAINS

But sizable numbers of Negroes remain apathetic. In the 2 for 1 Bar at 135th Street and Eighth Avenue, a man sitting at the bar was asked whether he thought he would profit from the current rights battle.

"I don't know nothing 'bout that," he replied. "All I want is another bottle of beer."

"All this hollering over integration don't mean nothing to me," a Negro laundry worker comments. "All them Negroes who are doing it hope to git something for themselves. All this stuff don't help people like me. I'm going to be working in a laundry all my life and there's no way to git out of it."

The despair and hopelessness of many Negroes is shown in other ways. Though there are some 400,000 Negroes packed into Harlem, the N.A.A.C.P., foremost of the civil rights groups, has never had more than 25,000 members in the community.

When rights groups hold out-door rallies there are often as many Negroes standing around on nearby streets ignoring them as there are present at the rallies.

THE SEPARATIST GROUP

And there is the Negro element that regards the white man as so "evil" that the black man can never achieve integration in a white-dominated society.

It believes the Negro's redemption must be found in the separation of the races. It demands a Negro state, a separate Negro economy, and a separate Negro culture as the road to equality, independence and dignity.

This group includes the Black Muslims, led in this area by Malcolm X.

A modern version of Marcus Garvey's "Back-to-Africa" enterprise is operated from a Harlem bookstore owned by Lewis H. Michaux, president of the African Nationalists in America.

The Michaux bookstore, at 125th Street and Seventh Avenue, carries a sign identifying it as "Repatriation Headquarters" for the

"Back-to-Africa Movement." It invites interested persons to come in to register or get information on the movement.

MOST WANT INTEGRATION

But almost invariably, Negroes talked to in The Times survey insisted they did not seek separation from whites but wanted — as Maude Blair, a Greenwich Village maid, put it — "to live as Americans in America and as Christians in a Christian country."

The victories in the drive for integration increase the impetus for more demonstrations.

"If they could not see success in sight, if there were no hope," says Mr. Randolph, "there would be no demonstrations. People without hope don't fight. If we stopped they'd think we were contented."

All of the civil rights officials interviewed — and most persons questioned on the streets — conceded that Negroes had made impressive gains on the national, states and local levels.

They noted that President Kennedy, Governor Rockefeller and Mayor Wagner had stepped up their programs to insure equal opportunity in jobs, schools, housing and other areas. They observed that the local building-trade unions seemed prepared to make concessions. They found the same true of private employers whose premises had been picketed.

The integrationists contend that, despite past efforts on the civil rights front, the slums are spreading, unemployment is rising in some categories, the schools do not seem to be improving at a fast enough pace and general frustration is increasing rapidly.

Will the frustration, disillusion and despair result in a violent collision between whites and Negroes?

Some Negro leaders predict that this will happen unless their people's demands are met quickly.

The Rev. Dr. Gardner C. Taylor, a Baptist minister who led the first demonstrations at the Downstate Medical Center in Brooklyn, has warned that "blood may flow in the streets" if the grievances of the Negroes are not removed.

But — like other Negro leaders — he quickly adds that the demonstrators will not initiate any violence. All provocations to violence, he asserts, will be made by the police or by opponents of Negro rights.

"We must insist on nonviolence," says Mr. Randolph. "Violence, even when practiced by the majority, has not worked." We are the proof of that, since it often has been used against Negroes. But it didn't stop us."

But all those who are active in staging the demonstrations are growing more keenly aware that it takes only one or two hotheads on either side of the picket line to set off a chain reaction of violence.

The major civil rights organizations, including the N.A.A.C.P., the Urban League and CORE, aware that wildcat demonstrators could provoke bloodshed, have begun coordinating their activities to keep better control over them.

In addition, the nonviolent nature of demonstrations acts as a safety valve.

REVOLUTION CALLED PEACEFUL

"We're not fighting a military battle. We're not trying to overthrow the government. This is a peaceful revolution," explain the Urban League's national executive director Whitney Young Jr.

Moreover, a steady procession of whites is joining the protest demonstrations, thus giving concrete expression of their sympathy for the Negro's cause.

So many whites are taking part in some demonstrations, in fact, that at one picketing site the other day a CORE leader pleaded with photographers not to take pictures "until we get some more Negroes on the line."

Some Negroes have grumbled that "whites are taking over our movement." But an over-whelming number of Negroes interviewed welcomed white participation as exhibiting the spirit of "true brotherhood." They note that the civil rights organizations have always been interracial in character.

Another safety valve is the fact that the police, though criticized by a few, have won praise for the gentle manner in which they handle the demonstrators they take to jail.

COMMISSIONER'S RULES

Police Commissioner Michael J. Murphy has insisted that the demonstrators be allowed to picket and protest. But he has been equally insistent that they not be permitted to block entrances to buildings or work projects.

Still another consideration that would help avert mass violence is this: There is far less resistance to the Negro's demands here than in the South. Pickets at a White Castle hamburger stand were pelted with stones and beer cans, but most whites have chosen to ignore the demonstrators and keep their opinions to themselves.

Also, elected officials here are extremely sensitive to the growing strength of the Negro vote in the city and state.

Moreover, a better moral climate exists in the metropolitan area, as far as civil rights are concerned, than exists in many parts of the South, Middle West or Far West.

Recently, for example, Cardinal Spellman of the Roman Catholic Archdiocese of New York and Bishop Bryan J. McEntegart of the Brooklyn Diocese issued vigorous statements urging racial justice for Negroes. This is in a city where Catholics make up a heavy proportion of the population.

Similar strong stands have been taken by Protestant and Jewish leaders, some of whom have joined the picket lines. Moreover, the city's newspapers and other communications media have, almost without exception, given strong support to the integration drive.

When the criticism is made that some demonstrations are irrational and inconvenience many people, James Farmer of CORE replies:

"Well, the Negro has been inconvenienced for a hundred years. We feel these demonstrations are necessary to dramatize the need for corrective measures."

PREFERENCES SOUGHT

The Urban League's Mr. Young has proposed a program of preferential treatment for Negroes to enable them to catch up with whites in jobs, education and housing.

Aware that his plan is controversial, Mr. Young argues that: "White people have had special preference all along, though they won't admit it. They've hired the white man, though the Negro might have been as qualified or better qualified. It's time we instituted a program of special treatment for Negroes as compensation for generations of denial, at least for a while."

"If a Negro and a white man of equal ability apply for a job the Negro should be hired." Mr. Young contends. "The Negro has been deliberately kept out of the mainstream of jobs, education and housing. He's been excluded for so long we need a crash program to include him."

"There's a simple way to stop all these protests and all these court actions and all these demonstrations," he went on. "That way is to grant the demands of the protestors."

"The Negro's demands are, after all, very modest," he observed. "They are asking for the right to get into apprenticeship programs, for the right to try a hamburger, for decent schools and decent housing. They are only asking for things that white people ask for — and get."

The Young plan of preferential treatment is drawing much favorable comment in the Negro community, though here and there a Negro is heard to complain that it makes it appear that Negroes have to be babied.

Mr. Young reports that his program frequently meets resistance from white employers, but that when it is explained to them, some actually begin to give preferential treatment to Negroes.

RECRUITING DONE

"Some of them," he notes, are hiring a higher proportion of Negroes than whites and are even making a special effort to recruit Negroes."

Another controversial plan is the quota system. Some CORE pickets, as well as other persons, have demanded that Negroes and Puerto

Ricans be given 25 per cent of all jobs at the companies they picket.

This figure is based on the premise that Negroes and Puerto Ricans make up about 25 per cent of the city's total population of nearly 8,000,000.

Although this plan is winning favor in some quarters in Negro and Puerto Rican communities, it is being resisted in others.

Some civil rights officials privately concede that the 25 per cent quota would be impractical on jobs requiring highly skilled workers because there might be difficulty in recruiting that many skilled Negro and Puerto Rican workers.

But they note that part of their purpose is to make employers and unions compensate for past injustices to the Negro.

Moreover, the civil rights groups say they want concessions that will guarantee that unions and management will never be able to go back to their old discriminatory ways.

"How many Negroes do you think are going to train for jobs they know they can't get?" is the way one put it.

The drive for Puerto Rican rights has developed recently as an adjunct of the general campaign for the "total elimination" of segregation and discrimination against the Negro.

PUERTO RICANS IN AREA

Though the Negro and Puerto Rican communities generally go their own ways and have little contact with each other, Negro and white civil rights leaders say that whatever gains are won by the Negro will also benefit the Puerto Rican, a more recent migrant to the metropolitan area.

There are about 800,000 Puerto Ricans in the metropolitan area. They have generally remained aloof from demonstrations, although a few have joined picket lines.

As the summer wears on, the voices of protest rise higher. The integrationist forces are stepping up their picketing, sit-ins and rallies. At the same time, thousands are attending similar rallies in Harlem and Brooklyn to hear the Black Muslims denounce the white man and demand separation of the races.

Many integrationists scoff at the program of the Muslims and the nationalists and contend that the increasing surge of the integration movement is cutting the ground out from under the segregation forces, white or black.

RIGHTS OF THE MUSLIMS

But some ardent integrationists back the fight of the Muslims and others to preach and practice racial separation and their own brand of "racial purity" and to make plans for the establishment of a Black Zion.

Ernest E. Johnson, a Harlem insurance man who has long supported integrationist causes puts it this way:

"We've got to recognize that the Negro community is not monolithic — economically, socially, or politically. There is room for the leftists, the rightists and the moderates. And there's a place for the Muslims and any other group that desires racial separation."

"The black man doesn't necessarily want integration," says James Lawson, head of the United African Nationalist Movement. "He wants justice and fair play."

THE END AND THE MEANS

But the overwhelming sentiment among Negros interviewed is that integration means justice and fair play, and that that is how the Negro's historical second-class status will be finally erased.

And for the present, the general Negro community continues to be swept along, and at any ever-increasing tempo, on the wave of the integration movement.

A Negro lawyer received a call from his 12-year-old daughter the other day. "Daddy, daddy," she cried. "I've been picketing." She had been picketing a decision by playground officials to close the area earlier than usual.

Thus has the protest movement spread like fire through the Negro community.

"I Have a Dream"

BY JAMES RESTON | AUG. 29, 1963

WASHINGTON, AUG. 28 — Abraham Lincoln, who presided in his stone temple today above the children of the slaves he emancipated, may have used just the right words to sum up the general reaction to the Negro's massive march on Washington. "I think," he wrote to Gov. Andrew G. Curtin of Pennsylvania in 1861, "the necessity of being ready increases. Look to it." Washington may not have changed a vote today, but is a little more conscious tonight of the necessity of being ready for freedom. It may not "look to it" at once, since it is looking to so many things, but it will be a long time before it forgets the melodious and melancholy voice of the Rev. Dr. Martin Luther King Jr. crying out his dreams to the multitude.

It was Dr. King who, near the end of the day, touched the vast audience. Until then the pilgrimage was merely a great spectacle. Only those marchers from the embattled towns in the Old Confederacy had anything like the old crusading zeal. For many the day seemed an adventure, a long outing in the late summer sun — part liberation from home, part Sunday School picnic, part political convention, and part fish-fry.

But Dr. King brought them alive in the late afternoon with a peroration that was an anguished echo from all the old American reformers. Roger Williams calling for religious liberty, Sam Adams calling for political liberty, old man Thoreau denouncing coercion, William Lloyd Garrison demanding emancipation, and Eugene V. Debs crying for economic equality — Dr. King echoed them all.

"I have a dream," he cried again and again. And each time the dream was a promise out of our ancient articles of faith: phrases from the Constitution, lines from the great anthem of the nation, guarantees from the Bill of Rights, all ending with a vision that they might one day all come true.

FIND JOURNEY WORTHWHILE

Dr. King touched all the themes of the day, only better than anybody

Martin Luther King Jr. acknowledging the crowd from the Lincoln Memorial during the March on Washington.

else. He was full of the symbolism of Lincoln and Gandhi, and the cadences of the Bible. He was both militant and sad, and he sent the crowd away feeling that the long journey had been worthwhile.

This demonstration impressed political Washington because it combined a number of things no politician can ignore. It had the force of numbers. It had the melodies of both the church and the theater. And it was able to invoke the principles of the founding fathers to rebuke the inequalities and hypocrisies of modern American life.

There was a paradox in the day's performance. The Negro leaders demanded equality "now," while insisting that this was only the "beginning" of the struggle. Yet it was clear that the "now," which appeared on almost every placard on Constitution Avenue, was merely an opening demand, while the exhortation to increase the struggle was what was really on the leaders' minds.

The question of the day, of course, was raised by Dr. King's theme:

Was this all a dream or will it help the dream come true?

No doubt this vast effort helped the Negro drive against discrimination. It was better covered by television and the press than any event here since President Kennedy's inauguration, and, since indifference is almost as great a problem to the Negro as hostility, this was a plus.

None of the dreadful things Washington feared came about. The racial hooligans were scarce. Even the local Nazi, George Lincoln Rockwell, minded his manners, which is an extraordinary innovation for him. And there were fewer arrests than any normal day for Washington, probably because all the saloons and hootch peddlers were closed.

POLITICIANS ARE IMPRESSED

The crowd obviously impressed the politicians. The presence of nearly a quarter of a million petitioners anywhere always makes a Senator think. He seldom ignores that many potential votes, and it did not escape the notice of Congressmen that these Negro organizations, some of which had almost as much trouble getting out a crowd as the Washington Senators several years ago, were now capable of organizing the largest demonstrating throng ever gathered at one spot in the District of Columbia.

It is a question whether this rally raised too many hopes among the Negroes or inspired the Negroes here to work harder for equality when they got back home. Most observers here think the latter is true, even though all the talk of "Freedom NOW" and instant integration is bound to lead to some disappointment.

The meetings between the Negro leaders on the one hand and President Kennedy and the Congressional leaders on the other also went well and probably helped the Negro cause. The Negro leaders were careful not to seem to be putting improper pressure on Congress. They made no specific requests or threats, but they argued their case in small groups and kept the crowd off Capitol Hill.

Whether this will win any new votes for the civil rights and economic legislation will probably depend on the over-all effect of the day's events on the television audience.

THE MAJOR IMPONDERABLE

This is the major imponderable of the day. The speeches were varied and spotty. Like their white political brethren, the Negroes cannot run a political meeting without letting everybody talk. Also, the platform was a bedlam of moving figures who seemed to be interested in everything except listening to the speaker. This distracted the audience.

Nevertheless, Dr. King and Roy Wilkins, head of the National Association for the Advancement of Colored People, and one or two others got the message across. James Baldwin, the author, summed up the day succinctly. The day was important in itself, he said, and "what we do with this day is even more important."

He was convinced that the country was finally grappling with the Negro problem instead of evading it; that the Negro himself was "for the first time" aware of his value as a human being and was "no longer at the mercy of what the white people imagine the Negro to be."

MERELY THE BEGINNING

On the whole, the speeches were not calculated to make Republican politicians very happy with the Negro. This may hurt, for, without substantial Republican support, the Kennedy program on civil rights and jobs is not going through.

Apparently this point impressed President Kennedy, who listened to some of the speeches on television. When the Negro leaders came out of the White House, Dr. King emphasized that bipartisan support was essential for passage of the Kennedy civil rights program.

Aside from this, the advantages of the day for the Negro cause outran the disadvantages. Above all, they got over Lincoln's point that "the necessity of being ready increases." For they left no doubt that this was not the climax of their campaign for equality but merely the beginning, that they were going to stay in the streets until they could get equality in the schools, restaurants, houses and employment agencies of the nation, and that, as they demonstrated here today, they had found an effective way to demonstrate for changes in the laws without breaking the law themselves.

Birmingham Bomb Kills 4 Negro Girls in Church; Riots Flare; 2 Boys Slain

BY CLAUDE SITTON | SEPT. 16, 1963

BIRMINGHAM, ALA., SEPT. 15 — A bomb severely damaged a Negro church today during Sunday school services, killing four Negro girls and setting off racial rioting and other violence in which two Negro boys were shot to death.

Fourteen Negroes were injured in the explosion. One Negro and five whites were hurt in the disorders that followed.

Some 500 National Guardsmen in battle dress stood by at armories here tonight, on orders of Gov. George C. Wallace. And 300 state troopers joined the Birmingham police, Jefferson County sheriff's deputies and other law-enforcement units in efforts to restore peace.

Governor Wallace sent the guardsmen and the troopers in response to requests from local authorities.

Sporadic gunfire sounded in Negro neighborhoods tonight, and small bands of residents roamed the streets. Aside from the patrols that cruised the city armed with riot guns, carbines and shotguns, few whiles were seen.

FIRE BOMB HURLED

At one point, three fires burned simultaneously in Negro sections, one at a broom and mop factory, one at a roofing company and a third in another building. An incendiary bomb was tossed into a supermarket, but the flames were extinguished swiftly. Fire marshals investigated blazes at two vacant houses to see if arson was involved.

Mayor Albert Beutwell and other city officials and civic leaders appeared on television station WAPI late tonight, and urged residents to cooperate in ending "this senseless reign of terror."

Sheriff Melvin Bailey referred to the day as "the most distressing in the history of Birmingham."

The explosion at the 16th Street Baptist Church this morning brought hundreds of angry Negroes pouring into the streets. Some attacked the police with stones. The police dispersed them by firing shotguns over their heads.

Johnny Robinson, a 16-year-old Negro, was shot in the back and killed by a policeman with a shotgun this afternoon. Officers said the victim was among a group that had hurled stones at white youths driving through the area in cars flying Confederate battle flags.

When the police arrived, the youths fled, and one policeman said he had fired low but that some of the shot had struck the Robinson youth in the back.

Virgil Wade, a 13-year-old Negro, was shot and killed just outside Birmingham while riding a bicycle. The Jefferson County sheriff's office said "there apparently was no reason at all" for the killing, but indicated that it was related to the general racial disorders.

Another Negro youth and a white youth were shot but not seriously wounded in separate incidents. Four whites, including a honeymooning couple from Chicago, were injured by stones while driving through the neighborhood of the bombing.

The bombing, the fourth such incident in less than a month, resulted in heavy damage to the church, to a two-story office building across the street and to a home.

WALLACE OFFERS REWARD

Governor Wallace, at the request of city officials, offered a $5,000 reward for the arrest, and conviction of the bombers.

None of the 50 bombings of Negro property here since World War II have been solved.

Mayor Boutwell and Chief of Police Jamie Moore expressed fear that the bombing, coming on top of tension aroused by desegregation of three schools last week, would bring further violence.

George G. Seibels Jr., chairman of the City Council's police committee, broadcast frequent appeals tonight to white parents, urging them to restrain their children from staging demonstrations tomorrow. He said that a repetition of the segregationist motorcades that raced through the streets last Thursday and Friday "could provoke serious trouble, resulting in possible death or injury."

The Rev. Dr. Martin Luther King Jr. arrived tonight by plane from Atlanta. He had led Negroes, who make up almost one-third of Birmingham's population, in a five-week campaign last spring that brought some lunch-counter desegregation and improved job opportunities. The bombed church had been used as the staging point by Negro demonstrators.

CURFEW PLAN REJECTED

Col. Albert J. Lingo, State director of Public Safety and commander of the troopers, met with Mayor Boutwell and the City Council in emergency session. They discussed imposition of a curfew, but decided against it.

The bombing came five days after the desegregation of three previously all-white schools in Birmingham. The way had been cleared for the desegregation when President Kennedy federalized the Alabama National Guard and the Federal courts issued a sweeping order against Governor Wallace, thus ending his defiance toward the integration step.

The four girls killed in the blast had just heard Mrs. Ella C. Demand, their teacher, complete the Sunday School lesson for the day. The subject was "The Love That Forgives."

During the period between the class and an assembly in the main auditorium, they went to the women's lounge in the basement, at the northeast corner of the church.

The blast occurred at about 10:25 A.M. (12:25 P.M. New York time).

Church members said they found the girls huddled together beneath a pile of masonry debris.

PARENTS OF 3 ARE TEACHERS

Both parents of each of three of the victims teach in the city's schools. The dead were identified by University Hospital officials as:

Cynthia Wesley, 14, the only child of Claude A. Wesley, principal of the Lewis Elementary School, and Mrs. Wesley, a teacher there.

Denise McNair, 11, also an only child, whose parents are teachers.

Carol Robertson, 14, whose parents are teachers and whose grandmother, Mrs. Sallie Anderson, is one of the Negro members of a biracial committee established by Mayor Boutwell to deal with racial problems.

Addie Mae Collins, 14, about whom no information was immediately available.

The blast blew gaping holes through walls in the church basement. Floors of offices in the rear of the sanctuary appeared near collapse. Stairways were blocked by splintered window frames, glass and timbers.

Chief Police Inspector W. J. Haley said the impact of the blast indicated that at least 15 sticks of dynamite might have caused it. He said the police had talked to two witnesses who reported having seen a car drive by the church, slow down and then speed away before the blast.

Civil Rights Victory

BY THE NEW YORK TIMES | FEB. 11, 1964

Proposed in 1963, the Civil Rights Act of 1964 ended segregation in public places and outlawed discrimination based on race, color, religion, sex or national origin.

PASSAGE OF THE Civil Rights Act of 1963 by The House of Representatives is a victory for the Administrations of President Kennedy and President Johnson, for the coalition of liberal Democrats and Republicans who steered the measure through the shoals of amendment and — lest it be forgotten — for millions of Americans deprived of a full life because of racial discrimination.

What the House leadership recognized during lengthy committee hearings and during the voting the last two weeks was that rights are indivisible. The right to register and vote in a national election cannot be separated from the right of equal opportunity to get a job; the right to compel desegregation of public schools for the benefit of children cannot be separated from the right to compel service in a restaurant or hotel for the benefit of their parents.

The sum of these rights and freedoms, without deductions, is what we recognize as citizenship. Where these rights are undercut, there democracy is that much less effective.

That articulate Negro spokesman, James Baldwin, is fond of saying, "Civil rights isn't a Negro problem — it's a white problem." The action in the House yesterday recognized the truth of that aphorism. Without regard to race, the victory can be shared by all Americans.

Incident at Selma

BY THE NEW YORK TIMES | MARCH 9, 1965

THE "BLOODY SUNDAY" in Selma, Ala., brings the moral and legal issues in that state once again to a point of crisis.

The right of citizens to assemble peacefully and to petition their elected officials for redress of their grievances is as old as free government and as plain as the Declaration of Independence. The state of Alabama has the responsibility to protect its citizens, both Negro and white, in the exercise of that right.

Gov. George C. Wallace has instead chosen to meet peaceful protest with armed force. By authorizing state troopers, sheriff's deputies and members of a volunteer posse to attack a group of private citizens, he has written another shameful page in his own record and in the history of Alabama.

The scene in Selma resembled that in a police state. Heavily armed men attacked the marchers. "The first ten or twenty Negroes were swept to the ground screaming, arms and legs flying." Tear gas was used. "Fifteen or twenty nightsticks could be seen through the gas, flailing at the heads of the marchers." The hurried rout went on. "Four or five women lay on the grass strip where the troopers had knocked them down." Witnesses "said they saw posse men using whips on the fleeing Negroes as they re-crossed the bridge."

If this is described as law enforcement, it is misnamed. It is nothing more nor less than race-conscious officialdom run amuck. It disgraces not only the state of Alabama but every citizen of the country in which it can happen.

Dr. King Deplores 'Long Cold Winter' On the Rights Front

BY THE NEW YORK TIMES | JUNE 20, 1967

"EVERYONE IS WORRYING about the long hot summer with its threat of riots," the Rev. Dr. Martin Luther King Jr. said yesterday. "We had a long cold winter when little was done about the conditions that create riots."

The civil rights leader and Nobel Peace Prize winner made this comment yesterday in discussing his book, "Where Do We Go From Here: Chaos or Community?" at a luncheon given for him by Harper & Row at Sardi's to mark the publication of the book.

"There has to be a long-range commitment by the nation," he continued. "Economic deprivation, the slums, the terribly inadequate schools — These are the problems that must be dealt with. Riots will not be stopped by the sermons of Martin Luther King. Nor by programs got up as we see summer approaching."

Dr. King said he would spend his summer in Cleveland and Chicago. He plans to work on the organization of tenants, on negotiating with industries to end racial discrimination or face boycotts, on representation for welfare recipients and on political and voter registration drives.

He indicated that he had written the book because he had come to feel last year he needed to "get a new sense of direction as to where we are in the basic problem."

The Ghetto Explodes in Another City

BY THE NEW YORK TIMES | JULY 16, 1967

IT WAS NEWARK'S turn last week.

The pattern of racial violence that has scarred city after city across the nation, leaving in its wake the debris-littered streets, the burned and looted shops, the dead and the injured — and always new legacies of hatred and bitterness — came to the city of 405,000, a 20-minute bus ride across the Hudson River from New York.

By late last night, as National Guardsmen, state troopers and helmeted policemen patrolled the torn streets of Newark's Central Ward — the Negro ghetto — the toll rose to more than 20 dead, with over 1,100 injured and over 1,600 arrested, and property damage in the millions.

But the even larger toll was starkly defined by New Jersey Gov. Richard J. Hughes who said Newark was a city in the grip of a "criminal insurrection" — a state of "open rebellion." Perhaps even more succinct was the comment of one National Guardsman who said: "This is just like two countries fighting."

It is the "two countries" that has always been at the heart of the violence that exploded in Harlem and Bedford-Stuyvesant in New York in 1964, in the Watts district of Los Angeles in 1965, in Chicago's West Side and Cleveland's Hough in 1966, and in Cincinnati, Buffalo, Boston, Hartford, Waterloo, Iowa and a score of other communities this spring and "long hot summer" whose end is not yet in sight.

There is the country of the whites — relatively prosperous, unencumbered for the most part by insurmountable social and economic barriers, free to shape its own destiny.

And then there is the country of the Negroes — a country whose capital is the ghetto, whose constitution states that "all men are created equal, but Whitey comes first," and whose statistics still spell out a largely unchanging picture, despite new laws on the books, of higher unemployment than the whites, poorer education, poorer housing, poorer — you name it.

MAYOR'S PREDICTION

"I do not believe there will be any mass violence in Newark this summer," said Mayor Hugh J. Addonizio last May. The Mayor, a Democrat and former Congressman with a liberal voting record on civil rights and other issues, was not being a blind Pollyanna. Newark, half of whose population is Negro — the largest proportion of any city in the North — had been comparatively free of serious racial trouble. Mayor Addonizio, with some justification, credited efforts by his administration at improved community relations as a factor.

But the Mayor — like other mayors has been struggling to cope with a growing low-income population. In 1950, the city had the highest proportion of dilapidated housing in the nation. A slum clearance program has helped somewhat, but it has barely touched the worst ghetto — the Central Ward.

In recent months, Newark's Negro community has been agitated by efforts by city officials to clear some 50 acres in a shabby Negro neighborhood for the site of the State College of Medicine and Dentistry. They have also been protesting about the rising unemployment among ghetto residents, and about an attempt to appoint a white City Councilman to a post on the Board of Education, rather than a Negro now serving as the city's budget director.

The explosion when it came was touched off — as has so often been the case in racial riots — by a relatively minor incident.

Last Wednesday, Negroes gathered at the Fourth Precinct station house to protest the alleged beating of a Negro taxi driver by police. Tempers rose, and the demonstrators let fly a hail of stones and bottles that broke almost every window in the police station.

Then the violence spread as Negro youths roamed the streets, smashed windows and looted stores, and hurled rocks at police.

On Thursday the rampaging grew worse. Negroes, some now

armed, firebombed stores, battled with firemen trying to control the blazes, and took up positions on rooftops to exchange shots with police. In the early hours of Friday morning, Mayor Addonizio, declaring the situation "ominous," telephoned Governor Hughes for National Guard reinforcements.

About 2,600 National Guardsmen rolled into the city in convoys of jeeps and trucks. But the sniper fire, the violence and the fury mounted, and hospital emergency rooms were soon overloaded with scores of injured persons, many in critical condition.

At times, amidst the scenes of riot and destruction that made parts of the city look like a battlefield, there was an almost carnival atmosphere. Negro housewives calmly invaded shops and supermarkets that did not bear signs saying "Soul Brother" — a kind of password among Negroes during the riot — and walked off with everything they could carry. Said one woman as she lifted bread off a supermarket shelf: "The brother's got to take everything he gets. Whitey ain't about to get up off of anything unless you make him."

Nearby, several teen-agers danced and laughed in the street as two of them held aloft sticks with yellow wigs on them. "We've scalped the white man!" they shouted. Governor Hughes, touring the shattered city, said bitterly, "It's like laughing at a funeral."

It was a wild and violent funeral of sorts as the Governor, the Mayor, and other officials sought yesterday to restore law and order. "The line between the jungle and the law might as well be drawn here as well as any place in America," Governor Hughes said.

But that was only one line. Beyond it lay other lines against which the Negro is pressing with ever-increasing force and impatience, precipitating in return a sharp white backlash. The struggle has riven the civil rights movement itself, with the militant "black power" elements increasingly challenging the moderates to act now and act strong because the waiting has been too long.

Marriage Curbs By States Scored

BY FRED P. GRAHAM | **APRIL 11, 1967**

The landmark Supreme Court decision on June 12, 1967, invalidated laws
prohibiting interracial marriage.

WASHINGTON, APRIL 10 — The Supreme Court was told today that statutes
prohibiting intermarriages between whites and Negroes were "slavery laws" held over from a bygone era.

An attorney for the American Civil Liberties Union compared Virginia's antimiscegenation laws with the laws of Nazi Germany and
South Africa and urged the Justices to strike down the system of statutes that dates back to 1691.

The attorney, Philip J. Hirschkop, of Alexandria, Va., said Virginia's laws denied Negroes the equal protection of the laws guaranteed
by the 14th Amendment. "They are slavery laws, pure and simple —
the most odious of the segregation laws," he said.

A Supreme Court ruling invalidating the Virginia law would have
the effect of voiding similar antimiscegenation laws in 15 other states.
They are: Alabama, Arkansas, Delaware, Florida, Georgia, Kentucky,
Louisiana, Mississippi, Missouri, North Carolina, Oklahoma, South
Carolina, Tennessee, Texas and West Virginia.

In more than two hours of argument today, in which almost every
member of the Court took part, no statement from the bench suggested
that the antimiscegenation laws might be constitutionally valid.

Assistant Attorney General R. D, McIlwaine 3d of Virginia leaned
heavily on the argument that none of the framers of the 14th Amendment intended to outlaw statutes against racial intermarriage. "If any
had suggested this, it would not have passed," he said.

Mr. McIlwaine contended that states have the power to outlaw marriage
between the races, as they have to pass laws against polygamy and incest.

He argued that Virginia's "strong policy" against interracial marriage was based upon firm scientific evidence. As proof he waved a thick volume entitled "Intermarriage — Interfaith, Interracial, Interethnic," by Dr. Albert I. Gordon.

Mr. McIlwaine cited statements by Dr. Gordon that interracial marriages were often contracted by rebellious individuals to express their social hostility. He said that "the progeny are the martyrs" of such unions, and contended that the state had a legitimate interest in preventing them.

Mr. Hirschkop called the Virginia law "ludicrous" and said that the Legislature had never been able to define "Negro" or "white person."

DEFINITION OFTEN CHANGED

He said the Legislature had changed the definition of a "Negro" from a person with one-eighth Negro blood in 1705 to one-fourth Negro blood in 1785, and to "any trace of Negro blood" in 1930. The present definition of a white person is one who has "no trace of any blood other than Caucasian."

The present case involves Richard Perry Loving, 33 years old, a white construction worker. His wife, Mildred, 27, is part Indian and part Negro.

They were given a year's prison sentence under two laws that make it a crime for a white Virginian to go out of the state to marry a Negro in an attempt to avoid the law against mixed marriages within the state.

A central issue in today's arguments was whether the Supreme Court could strike down the entire system of Virginia's antimiscegenation laws, or merely the criminal penalties invoked against the Lovings.

Mr. Hirschkop noted that the criminal penalty applies only to whites who marry Negroes. It does not touch on marriages between other racial groups.

But another Virginia law declares void any marriage between a white person and a person of any other race, said William M. Marutani, a lawyer from Philadelphia, who argued as a friend of the court for the Japanese American Citizens League.

He asked the Court to declare this law invalid along with the penal statutes as part of the same system. There are 1,750 Japanese in Virginia, according to census figures.

Slaying Recalls Series of Deaths That Have Marked Rights Fight

BY SETH S. KING | APRIL 5, 1968

IN ALBANY, GA., in 1962, the. Rev. Dr. Martin Luther King Jr. was preaching in a small church after shots were fired into nearby houses.

"It may get me crucified," he said. "I may even die. But I want it said even if I die in the struggle that 'He died to make me free.' "

Dr. King's death at the hands of a gunman in Memphis yesterday recalled those words. His death also recalled the series of racial slayings and shootings that began soon afterward and have recurred every year since then.

The first came a year later, in April, 1963. William L. Moore, a white mailman from Baltimore, was making a one-man march through the South to protest racial segregation. He was shot to death at close range as he walked one evening near the northeastern Alabama town of Attalla.

Two months later, Medgar W. Evers, Mississippi Field Secretary of the National Association for the Advancement of Colored People, was shot to death as he stepped out of his automobile in the driveway of his home in Jackson, Miss.

In the summer of 1964 hundreds of young civil rights workers from cities in the East and North converged on Mississippi to lead a drive to register Negroes to vote.

The nation was shocked in August by the disappearance of two young men from New York and their Negro companion. After an intensive search that lasted two weeks, the bullet-riddled bodies of Andrew Goodman, a student at Queens College; Michael H. Schwerner, a New York social worker, and James E. Chaney, a Negro civil rights worker from Meridian, were found in a shallow grave near that Mississippi town.

Early in 1965 the racial tensions that had been building burst forth in a bizarre direction.

Malcolm X, the fiery former supporter of Elijah Muhammed, the

Black Muslim leader, was speaking in the Audubon Ballroom on Broadway in Harlem when three Negroes charged down the aisle. A blast from a sawed-off shotgun hit the black militant, who died soon afterward.

At that time, Dr. King said: "I have learned to face threats on my life philosophically and have prepared myself for anything that might come." A month later he was at the head of his now famous march in Selma, Ala. Within a week three persons who had participated in it were dead from violence.

Jimmie Lee Jackson, a young Negro marcher, was the first. He was shot down in a cafe in nearby Marion.

Then the Rev. James L. Reeb, a Protestant minister from Boston, was beaten by a mob of white men in a Selma street and died a few days later.

Before the march ended the nation was again appalled when Mrs. Viola Gregg Liuzzo, a Detroit housewife who had left her husband and five children to help in the march, was shot to death while driving her car between Selma and Montgomery.

The summer of 1965 marked the death and critical wounding in Alabama of two more white men who went South to participate in civil rights work.

On Aug. 21, Jonathan Myrick Danials, a 26-year-old Episcopal seminarian from Keene, N. H., died from the blast of a shotgun as he walked to a grocery store with two Negro girls in Haynesville. A Roman Catholic priest, the Rev. Richard F. Morrisroe of Chicago, was critically wounded by the same blast.

The summer of 1966 saw the wounding of James H. Meredith, the first Negro to attend the University of Mississippi. He was injured by a blast fired from ambush along a country road near Hernando as he walked across the state to prove that a Negro civil rights leader could do so.

Early last year, as he was driving his truck home from work, Wharlest Jackson, treasurer of the N.A.A.C.P. branch in Natchez. Miss., was killed by a bomb thrown into the vehicle.

CHAPTER 4

One Step Forward, Two Steps Back

The power of the civil rights era drove racism underground. Schools were legally desegregated, but in reality are ever-more resegregated. The country elected its first black president, yet a disproportionate number of people of color are still killed by the police. And although the Supreme Court recently overruled the World War II call for Japanese internment, many believe it was done to off-set the court's decision to uphold President Trump's ban against citizens from several predominantly Muslim countries from entering the United States.

Desegregation Course Charted By Legal Unit After Bus Ruling

BY C. GERALD FRASER | APRIL 23, 1971

THERE WAS A TRACE of triumph in the room. A feeling that the war was not yet over, but that an important corner had been turned — a major battle won.

In the library of the N.A.A.C.P. Legal Defense and Educational Fund, Inc., 12 lawyers and staff members crowded behind a series of tables, surrounded by hundreds of law volumes.

They told how they hoped to end school segregation in all of the major urban areas of the South.

And they announced the start of a "substantial desegregation campaign" in medium-sized school districts in the North.

The fund is moving in the wake of decisions announced Tuesday by the Supreme Court in six cases, the key one being Swann et al. v. Charlotte-Mecklenburg Board of Education et al.

Jack Greenberg, director of the fund, said at a news conference yesterday at the headquarters, 10 Columbus Circle, that the decision meant that the concept of the neighborhood school was no longer "sacrosanct."

In the numerous cases pending all over the South, Mr. Greenberg said, judges will be asked to order desegregation. The fact that the Swann decision declared busing could be used to implement desegregation and that judges could examine black/white pupil ratios in schools to determine the effectiveness of desegregation plans left few foreseeable obstacles in the way of a desegregated Southern educational system.

Norman Chachkin, a staff lawyer, said fund cases were pending in Little Rock, North Little Rock, El Dorado and West Memphis, Ark.; Atlanta, Macon, Columbus and Albany, Ga.; Lake Charles, Opelousas and Shreveport, La.; and "all the major cities of Tennessee."

Also, Houston and Fort Worth, Tex.; Montgomery, Birmingham, Huntsville, Mobile, Tuscaloosa and Anniston, Ala.; Charleston, Greenville, S. C.; all cities in North Carolina; the big cities in Florida, except Miami; and Roanoake, Norfolk, Portsmouth and Newport News, Va.

What will they undertake first?

"You can't draw priorities anywhere," Mr. Chachkin said. "You can't pick out any cases and say they are more important than any other cases. We have never been able to find a way."

Jean Fairfax, director of the division of legal information and community services, said the fund would be concerned with two major areas: one, the existence of bad school desegregation plans — "a plan that does not work" — and two, "the compliance procedures for implementing the plans once they have been approved."

On Northern desegregation, she said the fund would focus on school districts "which we believe offer promise for becoming completely integrated systems .... school districts that have some of the same features as districts in the South."

Gerrymandered districts, districts with "optional zones" [where white children are permitted to transfer out], are going to be looked at very carefully," she said. Districts where she said the "burden" was on black children — where there is, for example, one-way busing — will also be scrutinized.

Mount Vernon, N.Y., Morristown, N.J., Denver, and Detroit are some of the Northern cities where the fund has begun court action.

Standing Up for Civil Rights

BY THE NEW YORK TIMES | MARCH 23, 1988

CONGRESS HAS WISELY and firmly turned back one of the most important political challenges to civil rights in recent years. The vote to override President Reagan's veto of the Civil Rights Restoration Act reconfirms a solid bipartisan consensus in Congress. It also catches the Reagan Administration, once again, on the wrong side of a civil rights issue.

A simple question sparked the confrontation between the White House and Congress: Should institutions that receive Federal money be forbidden to discriminate on the basis of race, sex, age or disability? In 1984, the Administration argued in the Grove City College case that Federal money flowing to one school department bound only that department to the anti-discrimination principle, and not the whole school.

Unfortunately, the Supreme Court accepted that argument, reversing years of legal understanding. It took four years — and the efforts of a determined, broad-based civil rights coalition — to secure passage of a bill that would simply restore several Federal civil rights laws to their pre-Grove City status. Throughout that process, the Administration insisted that the bill represented new, burdensome and inappropriate regulation. Other opponents of the bill wrongly characterized it as a gay rights bill, though it offers no new protection for homosexuals. Despite the widespread misinformation campaign, the Senate voted to override Mr. Reagan's veto by 73 to 24, and the House followed with a resounding 292-to-133 vote. The tallies demonstrated the strength of the bipartisan consensus that originally passed the bill.

An 'Aberration' or Police Business as Usual?

BY THE NEW YORK TIMES | MARCH 10, 1991

BLACK PEOPLE'S COMPLAINTS of police brutality have been made so often for so long that they seem almost part of the fabric of urban life, like homelessness and traffic jams. But like a storm gathering fury across a plain, reaction to the brutal beating of Rodney Glen King by a group of Los Angeles police officers swelled into a national outpouring of outrage last week as networks broadcast a videotape of the incident.

The tape, by an amateur photographer, showed this:

Fifteen police officers in 10 patrol cars stopped Mr. King's white sedan. As Mr. King lay on the ground offering no resistance, he was surrounded by officers, one of whom shocked him with a stun gun as others hit him more than 50 times with their batons and kicked him in the head and body at least seven times while he begged them to stop.

Police initially charged Mr. King with speeding and resisting arrest. But those charges were dropped after the police chief, Darryl F. Gates, conceded that the tape showed unnecessary force being used and said that some of the police involved would face charges instead. More than 1,000 callers from around the country phoned Mr. Gates's office expressing their outrage and demanding that he resign. So did local civil rights groups, saying that his history of controversial statements on race and drugs created an atmosphere conducive to police brutality.

Mr. Gates, whose job is protected by civil service regulations, said the beating was "an aberration" and that he would not resign. He also denied that racism was a factor in the beating of Mr. King, who is black.

Mr. King, who suffered a fractured eye socket, broken cheekbone, broken leg, facial nerve damage and a concussion, said that he and his wife would file suit against the police.

To some in Los Angeles, the whole affair came as no surprise. "It was horrible, but we receive complaints of this kind of conduct on a weekly basis," said Karol Heppe, head of the Police Misconduct Lawyers Referral Service. "The difference this time is that there was somebody there to videotape it."

Officer Says Beaten Man Resisted

BY SETH MYDANS | MARCH 31, 1991

A CALIFORNIA HIGHWAY PATROL officer has testified that a black motorist appeared to resist being handcuffed in the minutes just before he was beaten by white officers four weeks ago.

The officer, Melanie Singer, testified that the motorist, Rodney G. King, "wasn't punching at any one officer" as they tried to handcuff him.

"He was swinging wildly, pushing officers away," Officer Singer is quoted as saying in transcripts of a grand jury hearing released Friday. "Each officer had portions of his clothing, like his shirt. Two or three of them were trying to grab his wrists or hands, trying to get a hold of him. But like I say, he was moving in that little circle that they were in, trying to break loose of the circle."

Officer Singer's account was not supported by that of another witness, Josie S. Morales, who said that she watched the beating from across the road and that Mr. King "was laying very still" when "they started to hit him."

A videotape of the incident, made by an amateur photographer across the street, begins shortly after the officers began beating Mr. King.

Los Angeles Policemen Acquitted in Taped Beating

BY SETH MYDANS | APRIL 30, 1992

FOUR LOS ANGELES police officers were acquitted of assault today in the videotaped beating of a black motorist that stunned the nation. The verdicts immediately touched off a storm of anger and scattered violence in the city.

As residents set scores of fires, looted stores and beat passing motorists in the downtown area and pockets of predominantly black south-central Los Angeles, Mayor Tom Bradley declared a state of emergency, and Gov. Pete Wilson said he would send in the National Guard.

After hearing seven weeks of detailed testimony and studying the 81-second amateur videotape of the beating, the jury concluded that the policemen, all of whom are white, had not broken any laws when they clubbed and kicked the mostly prone motorist, Rodney G. King.

It was deadlocked on one of the 11 charges, and the prosecution said it might seek a new trial on that charge, which affected only one defendant.

The beating last spring, with its kicks and its 56 baton swings, was shown over and over on television. It immediately became one of the most visible uses of force by police in this country's history and put the issue of police brutality on the national agenda.

Immediately after the verdicts, an unusually impassioned Mayor Bradley appeared on television to appeal for calm in a city where the videotape has come to symbolize complaints about police brutality, racism and street violence.

"Today the system failed us," the Mayor said.

Despite Mr. Bradley's plea, street violence, looting and fires broke out in inner-city Los Angeles within hours of the verdicts. The Mayor called for the California National Guard to restore order and declared a local emergency. Governor Wilson ordered some units into the city, his spokesman said. Shortly after 11 P.M. Mayor Bradley said that he believed the scattered disturbances had been brought under control.

Although they, too, called for calm, community leaders expressed outrage that what had seemed on the videotape to be a clear-cut instance of police brutality had gone unpunished. The absence of blacks on the jury, picked from mostly white Ventura County about 45 miles northwest of Los Angeles after a change of venue to avoid pre-trial publicity, was used to enforce their allegations of racism.

The prosecutor, Deputy District Attorney Terry White, said the verdict "sends out a message that whatever you saw on that tape was reasonable conduct."

A QUICK DECISION

Jurors said it had taken only a day to reach their acquittals on the main charges against Sgt. Stacey C. Koon, 41 years old; Officers Laurence M. Powell, 29, and Theodore J. Briseno, 39; and former Officer Timothy E. Wind, 31. Jurors said that after six more days of deliberation they remained deadlocked on a charge against Officer Powell of use of excessive force. Mr. White said his office would seek a new trial on that charge, but prosecutors said later that they would reassess their plans. A hearing was set for May 15.

Late Wednesday night assistant United States Attorney General John R. Dunne said that the Justice Department, which monitored the trial, planned to review the case to see if any further action should be taken under Federal civil rights laws. The three officers have been suspended without pay since the beating and still face disciplinary hearings by the department; Mr. Wind, a rookie without tenure, was dismissed.

The four men were among two dozen officers who were present shortly after midnight on March 3, 1991, when Mr. King was stopped after a 15-minute high-speed chase, beaten, hogtied, thrown into an ambulance and sent to a hospital with multiple cuts and fractures. He was never charged in connection with the traffic stop.

The charges against the policemen included assault with a deadly weapon, excessive use of force as a police officer, filing a false report and acting as an accessory after the fact.

Jurors, 10 of whom are white, 1 Asian and 1 Hispanic, refused to be interviewed by reporters, issuing a brief statement that gave no indication of the basis on which they reached their verdicts.

Ted Koppel, the anchor of the ABC News program "Nightline," said he had interviewed a juror who declined to be identified on television and who had said that the video was weakened as a piece of evidence because Mr. King did not testify for the prosecution.

"The cops were simply doing what they'd been instructed to do," the juror was quoted as saying. "They were afraid he was going to run or even attack them."

Mr. Koppel said the juror criticized the video as unsteady and out of focus, and questioned the seriousness of Mr. King's injuries.

"A lot of those blows, when you watched them in slow motion, were not connecting," the juror was quoted as saying. "Those batons are heavy, but when you looked at King's body three days after the incident, not that much damage was done."

As a court officer read out 10 separate verdicts of not guilty, the defendants sat motionless and expressionless, as they have throughout most of the trial. Then they rose and embraced their lawyers.

'WHAT RACE ARE YOU?'

Loud arguments broke out between whites and blacks outside the courthouse.

"What race are you?" a black man shouted.

A white man yelled back, "I'm an American!"

The black man then shouted, "We're not judged as Americans!"

Stones were thrown at Officer Powell as he left the courthouse, said Sgt. Dick Southwick of the Ventura County Sherrif's Department. Angry groups of shouting spectators also confronted Mr. Wind and Sergeant Koon as they left the building.

After nightfall, more crowds gathered at police headquarters and City Hall, where they set a small fire in the lobby. Throughout the afternoon and into the night, young men in south-central Los Angeles smashed storefronts, set fire to shops and vehicles and pulled motorists from their cars and beat them. There were about 120 separate blazes, the Fire Department said.

As a news helicopter filmed one scene, a group stopped a car and beat the driver. Several men approached the driver and, one by one, kicked him and smashed bottles over his head.

A line of police cars, their lights flashing, approached cautiously as a nearby liquor store, surrounded by looters, burst into flame.

STRONG WORDS FROM MAYOR

In his news conference after the verdicts, Mayor Bradley, a former police officer, said, "The jury's verdict will never blind us to what we saw on that videotape. The men who beat Rodney King do not deserve to wear the uniform of the L.A.P.D."

The Los Angeles County District Attorney, Ira Reiner, whose office prosecuted the case, said: "We disagree with the jury, but are obliged to accept the integrity of that verdict. It's a time for sober reflection, not recrimination."

President Bush, who said last year that the videotape sickened him, also appealed for reason tonight, saying: "The court system has worked. What's needed now is calm, respect for the law."

Gov. Bill Clinton of Arkansas, the likely Democratic Presidential nominee, said, "Like most of America I saw the tape of the beatings several times, and it certainly looks excessive to me so I don't understand the verdict."

Willie L. Williams, who has been named to succeed Police Chief Darryl F. Gates, said, "There are obviously two camps operating out of Los Angeles, one that believes the police officers are guilty, one that they are totally innocent. And whether we like it or not, we have to accept the judicial process." Mr. Williams added that the verdict would make his new job "a little more challenging. It will place additional pressures on me and the department to convince the community that the Police Department is a fair institution ..."

The jury's verdicts flew in the face of the verdict of public opinion, which over the past year has condemned the videotaped beating as police brutality in its rawest form.

Police departments in other cities played the tape for their officers as a cautionary lesson. But many civil rights groups and black community leaders said Mr. King's beating was unusual only in that it had been captured on videotape.

As a result of the publicity, United States Attorney General Dick Thornburgh ordered a review of police-brutality complaints around the nation.

In Los Angeles, an independent commission headed by Warren M. Christopher, a Deputy Secretary of State in the Carter Adminstration, recommended broad changes in the Police Department. Under intense pressure, Chief Gates announced he would resign his tenured position, and although he has continued to hold onto office, his replacement, Willie L. Williams, the Philadelphia Police Commissioner, was announced this month.

The videotape was the central piece of evidence at the trial. As defense lawyers sought explanations for this or that baton swing or kick, the prosecutor urged jurors simply to watch the tape and to believe their eyes.

Arguing that Mr. King was making potentially threatening movements as he rolled on the ground under the blows, the defense brought experts in police procedures to testify about the propriety of the actions on the tape.

"If reasonable police minds could differ over the propriety of the use of force on March 3, 1991," the lawyer for Officer Powell, Michael P. Stone, told the jury, "then I suggest to you there is no proof beyond a reasonable doubt" that the beating was a criminal assault.

The prosecutor presented his own expert to testify that the beating was unjustified and countered that at some point each juror would find himself saying, "Enough is enough."

In their closing arguments, both sides focused on an issue at the heart of the controversy over the police department, what Mr. Christopher called its "siege mentality."

Defense lawyers referred repeatedly to the "thin blue line" and the role of a police force in protecting society from "the likes of Rodney King."

"This unpleasant incident is what we have police for," said Paul dePasquale, the lawyer for Mr. Wind. "The circumstances here were consistent with the job the man was hired to do. He was part of the line between society and chaos."

The videotape was shown repeatedly during the trial at slow, super-slow and normal speeds, with the roar of a police helicopter, the muffled shouts of the police and the occasional crack of a baton blow filling the courtroom.

Mr. King's lawyer, Steven Lerman, said his client did not appear as a witness because he had been confused and frightened since the beating and had problems with short-term memory.

Sergeant Koon, a 14-year veteran, is not shown on the tape hitting Mr. King but was being held responsible for the actions of the men under his command. He faced a maximum sentence of four years, eight months on charges of assault with a deadly weapon, using excessive force as a police officer, filing a false report and being an accessory after the fact.

He testified that Mr. King's erratic and uncooperative behavior after the traffic stop made it necessary to use force. "Sometimes police work is brutal. That's just a fact of life," he said.

Officer Powell is shown on the tape delivering most of the baton blows and was described by prosecutors as making racial slurs and laughing about the beating. He faced seven years and eight months on charges of assault, using excessive force as a police officer and filing a false report. He was also the subject of two special allegations of causing great bodily injury.

Mr. Wind, who was in training with Officer Powell, is shown on the tape delivering about 15 baton blows and several kicks. He faced a possible total of seven years on the same charges as Officer Powell, except for that of filing a false report.

Mr. dePasquale argued that his client was applying in textbook fashion the use-of-force techniques he had so recently learned in the police academy. "Watch Timothy Wind's posture: cautious, withdrawn, quick feet, sliding back, keeping moving, keeping clear but doing his job," he said. "This is not some orgy of violence. This is careful police work."

Officers in Bronx Fire 41 Shots, And an Unarmed Man Is Killed

BY MICHAEL COOPER | FEB. 5, 1999

The four police officers were acquitted of all charges, but the Diallo family received a settlement of $3 million from the City of New York.

AN UNARMED West African immigrant with no criminal record was killed early yesterday by four New York City police officers who fired 41 shots at him in the doorway of his Bronx apartment building, the police said.

It was unclear yesterday why the police officers had opened fire on the man at 12:44 A.M. in the vestibule of his building at 1157 Wheeler Avenue in the Soundview section. The man, Amadou Diallo, 22, who came to America more than two years ago from Guinea and worked as a street peddler in Manhattan, died at the scene, the police said.

The Bronx District Attorney's office is investigating the shooting, whose details were still murky last night because there were apparently no civilian witnesses and none of the police officers involved had given statements to investigators. But Inspector Michael Collins, a police spokesman, said that investigators who went to the scene of the shooting did not find a weapon on or near Mr. Diallo.

Relatives and neighbors described Mr. Diallo as a shy, hard-working man with a ready smile, a devout Muslim who did not smoke or drink.

"I am very angry," said his uncle, Mamadou Diallo. "He was a skinny guy. Why would the police shoot somebody of that nature 30 or 40 times? We see the police and we give them all the respect we have."

A friend, Demba Sanyang, 39, said: "We have a very undemocratic society back home, and then we come here. We don't expect to be killed by law enforcement officers."

The four officers involved in the shooting were assigned to the aggressive Street Crimes Unit, which focuses largely on taking illegal guns off the street. All four officers, who were in plainclothes, used their 9-millimeter semiautomatic service pistols, which hold 16 bullets and can discharge all of them in seconds. Two of the officers, Sean Carroll, 35, and Edward McMellon, 26, emptied their weapons, firing 16 shots each, the police said. Officer Kenneth Boss, 27, fired his gun five times and Officer Richard Murphy, 26, fired four times.

All four have been put on administrative leave, which is standard practice after a police shooting. Three of the officers — Officers Carroll, McMellon and Boss — have been involved in shootings before, which is unusual in a department where more than 90 percent of all officers never fire their weapons in the line of duty. In those previous incidents, Officers Carroll and McMellon were found to have acted properly, the police said; the case of Officer Boss — he shot and killed a man said to be armed with a shotgun on Oct. 31, 1997, in Brooklyn — is still being reviewed by the Brooklyn District Attorney's office.

Police rules on when officers can fire their guns are explicit: deadly force can be used only when officers fear for their lives or the lives of others. But once they decide to shoot, officers are trained to fire until they "stop" the target from causing harm. They are told not to fire warning shots, and to aim for the center of the body, not arms or legs.

Police officials said it was unclear whether the circumstances of the confrontation between Mr. Diallo and the officers justified such a shooting. What the police say is known is that the four officers were patrolling Mr. Diallo's neighborhood yesterday morning in an unmarked car in the hope that they would make arrests and in the process turn up information about a serial rapist in the area.

At a quarter to one, the officers encountered Mr. Diallo. All four got out of the car and approached him as he stood in the vestibule of his building, the police said.

A police official who spoke on the condition of anonymity said that a neighbor reported after the shooting that he had noticed a man, who the police believe was Mr. Diallo, loitering in the vestibule. The man described him as "acting suspicious," said the official, who did not elaborate.

The officers did not communicate over their radios before they approached Mr. Diallo, the police said, so investigators said they did not know what prompted their initial interest in him. Nor is it known why the officers began firing. A second police official who spoke on the condition of anonymity said, "We don't know what happened, because we haven't spoken to them, but it looks like one guy may have panicked and the rest followed suit."

After the shooting the officers called in on their radios, the police said, and neighbors telephoned 911. Soon other officers arrived on the scene, followed by detectives and the ranking officers who are required to respond to all police shootings.

An investigation began, and no weapon was found on Mr. Diallo, Inspector Collins said. A pager and a wallet were found lying next to the body, a police official said, adding that it was unclear whether the officers could have mistaken the pager for a weapon.

Mr. Diallo had lived in New York for two and a half years. A member of the Fulani ethnic group, he came from a village called Lelouma and followed relatives who had moved here. He worked as a street peddler, selling socks, gloves and videos on 14th Street in Manhattan. He sent much of the money he earned to his parents back home, friends said.

Yesterday, Mr. Diallo arrived home from work around midnight, said his roommate, Momodou Kujabi. The two men discussed who was going to pay the Con Edison bill, and then Mr. Diallo turned on the television and Mr. Kujabi went to bed. Another roommate, Mr. Diallo's cousin, Abdou Rahman Diallo, was already asleep.

Mr. Kujabi said he thought Mr. Diallo might have gone out for something to eat, as he often did after coming home from work. Then came the shots, and a knock on the door, he said. It was the police.

Mr. Kujabi said that the officers brought him down to the vestibule to identify his friend's body. "I said, 'How can this happen?' " Mr. Kujabi recalled telling the officers. " 'I left this guy less than 30 minutes ago.' "

An autopsy found that Mr. Diallo died of multiple gunshot wounds to the torso, said Ellen Borakove, a spokeswoman for the Chief Medical Examiner's Office. Further tests are required to learn how many wounds there were and where the bullets entered his body, she said.

Steven Reed, a spokesman for the Bronx District Attorney's office, said the shooting was being investigated would probably be taken up by a grand jury.

Stuart London, a lawyer representing the officers, said that he was still trying to determine the facts of the case. "It would be premature to comment," he said.

And Mayor Rudolph W. Giuliani urged people to withhold judgment on the case. "We've had terrible mistakes in this city when people have reacted to rumors and intuitions and feelings," he said. "Let's let the situation run its course and then let's react to the facts."

But Kyle Waters, a lawyer representing Mr. Diallo's family, said he was concerned that the police officers may have overreacted to Mr. Diallo. "There was nothing to indicate that he was a criminal, nothing to indicate that he had a weapon," he said. "For him to be sent back to his homeland in Guinea in a box is a horrible tragedy." State Assemblyman Ruben Diaz, who represents the area, called the shooting "outrageous," adding that it was clear that excessive force was used.

Mayor Giuliani said the circumstances of the shooting were unclear because the officers involved had invoked what is known as the 48-hour rule, which gives police officers two business days to consult with their union lawyers before they speak to investigators.

But police officials said that was not the case; instead, they said, they have not spoken to the officers because the Bronx District Attorney's office asked them not to. That is common practice in police shootings.

When prosecutors pursue possible criminal charges, police officers, like other citizens, can invoke their right against self-incrimination and decline to talk. The 48-hour rule comes into play when the Police Department pursues possible administrative charges. Officers in such an investigation are required to answer questions after the 48-hour respite, or face dismissal.

Yesterday, relatives began making plans to return the body of Mr. Diallo to his parents in the village of Lelouma. "I think there is no reason to shoot someone more than 30 times," said Mamadou Diallo.

Broader Palette Allows
for Subtler Census Portrait

BY ERIC SCHMITT | MARCH 12, 2001

HERNDON, VA. — When Fernando White was filling out last year's census form, one choice was easy. The son of a Salvadoran mother and an African-American father, Mr. White marked "Hispanic" as his ethnicity.

But a new option that allowed people to pick more than one racial category for the first time gave him pause. His mother is white, his father is black, but Mr. White says he considers himself an "Afro-Latino."

"I had to think twice about it and call a few friends to see what they put down," said Mr. White, 28, a community development worker who grew up in a black neighborhood in Washington, 25 miles east of here, and lives with his family on the outskirts of Herndon. He said he eventually picked "black" and "other."

The release last week of the first detailed 2000 census data for several states, including Virginia, revealed that this outer suburb has grown into an even more diverse place, in racial and ethnic terms, than it was a decade ago, mirroring a trend throughout the state and nation. Hispanics, for example, now make up 26 percent of the town's population, up from 10 percent in 1990, using adjusted census counts for that year. The town's Asian population increased to 13.9 percent from 8.4 percent.

But equally significant are alterations in the census itself. By allowing people to pick from among six racial choices — white, black, Asian, American Indian or Alaska native, Pacific Islander or Hawaiian native, or some other race — the 2000 census offers the most detailed portrait of the country's multiracial mix. For Herndon's 21,655 residents (up 32 percent from 1990), that means that the census represents a changing way of describing a changing town.

On Monday this new way of describing America's racial and ethnic makeup will be on display when the Census Bureau releases a detailed breakdown of the nation's racial complexion.

By permitting people to choose a host of racial options for themselves, the 2000 census presents a mosaic of 63 racial categories, compared with 5 a decade ago. Combine these racial classifications with two ethnic possibilities — Hispanic or non-Hispanic — and this tally produced a total of 126 racial and ethnic combinations.

Here in Herndon, 1,152 people or 5.3 percent of the population, said they belonged to two or more races, with 8 people saying they belonged to four or more. Overall in Fairfax County, 3.65 percent of the population identified with more than one race.

"The restrictions have been lifted on everyone so that people do not have to define themselves in a rigid way," said Edwin C. Darden, a board member of the Association of Multiethnic Americans who lives in nearby Springfield, Va.

The organization lobbied for the more nuanced set of racial categories to reflect more precisely the nation's growing levels of immigration and interracial marriages.

But some residents here expressed doubts that the government's effort to paint a more finely grained picture of America would capture how people actually view themselves.

Said Salah, 31, a pricing analyst who volunteers at the All Dulles Area Muslim Society, a makeshift mosque and Islamic education center here, said Arabs were generally considered by the government, and for census purposes, as white. But his Egyptian friends who are black clearly do not fit that definition, Mr. Salah said, and for them to mark both races would be misleading.

"The Census Bureau doesn't have it down to a science and never will," Mr. Salah said outside the center's second-floor prayer room, where more than 250 people attend Friday services. "The intent is good but will it achieve anything that's tangible?"

For Mr. Salah and Amina Chaudary, another volunteer instructor at the center, race takes a back seat to faith when it comes to self-identity.

"I define myself as a Muslim," said Ms. Chaudary, 22, who is applying to law schools. "To me that's what dominates my life."

Racial and ethnic changes have swept over Herndon, a once slow-paced dairy farming community named after an 19th-century sea captain, William Lewis Herndon.

Town officials say much of the growth in the last decade has been driven by the booming high technology corridor near Dulles International Airport, less than a mile away. The town's ample mix of moderate-income housing has attracted many immigrants and other newcomers.

"There's a good solid middle class in the town," said Anne Cahill, Fairfax County's chief demographer.

To see a tangible sign of the changing face of Herndon, just come early any morning to the corner of Elden Street and Alabama Drive, where scores of day laborers, largely from Central America, wait for construction bosses or cable installers to tap them for several hours of work.

Longtime white residents expressed mixed feelings about their town's shifting racial and ethnic character.

Alberta Payne, 78, was born and reared here when there were no stop lights downtown and her grandfather owned a 200-acre cattle farm that stretched all the way to the Potomac River. "I'm not sure it's all for the good," Mrs. Payne said. "We didn't have all the foreigners back then."

One of Dave Ballengee's biggest thrills in living here the last 28 years was seeing Muhammad Ali up close when the former boxing champion visited the Islamic education center a few years back. "Every culture is here, and I think it improves the quality of life," said Mr. Ballengee, 53, a cartographer who is white.

Aaron Sawyer, 51, an information-technology recruiter, moved here three years ago from Orange, N.J., to capitalize on one of his field's hottest markets. Mr. Sawyer, who is black, said he checked off the "non-Hispanic" and "black" boxes on the census, joining 1,999 other townspeople who checked the same categories.

Other blacks in Herndon, both Hispanic and non-Hispanic, took advantage of the new option to check off other racial categories to which they said they belong. For instance, 165 non-Hispanic blacks identified themselves with other races, as did 45 Hispanic blacks. In another piece of the Herndon mosaic, 96 non-Hispanic American Indians said they belonged to at least one other race, while 25 Hispanic American Indians said the same thing.

These numbers are relatively small, just as they are apt to be nationally, when the figures are released on Monday. Yet they add a slightly distinct flavor to communities formerly measured by traditional census methods.

At his town house, Mr. White's wife, Vanessa, 29, explained that she is Panamanian, has one grandparent from England, another from Italy and ancestors who are black.

As their two daughters, Calisa, 2, and Adina, 5, played in the living room, speaking alternately in Spanish and English, Mr. White observed: "When you combine what their mother's side brings and what I bring, tell me what they get? It's all a personal perception."

U.S. Schools Turn More Segregated, a Study Finds

BY DIANA JEAN SCHEMO | JULY 20, 2001

AS PRESIDENT BUSH and Congress wrestle with how to toughen federal law to weed out failing public schools, a Harvard University study has found that classrooms grew more segregated in the 1990's. The trend, reversing desegregation gains from the civil rights era, is undermining the educational prospects of black and Hispanic children, the study says.

The report, "Schools More Separate: Consequences of a Decade of Resegregation," by the university's Civil Rights Project, confirms a return toward segregation in the K-to-12 grades despite a growing diversity of the general population and support for integration in public opinion surveys.

It attributes the trend to court decisions limiting and reversing desegregation orders, a decline in federal support for desegregation, enduring housing segregation and demographic shifts.

The study, which analyzed educational and census data, found that 70 percent of black children attended predominantly minority schools in the 1998–99 academic year, up from 66 percent in 1991–92 and 63 percent in 1980–81. More than 36 percent were in "intensely minority" schools — those where 9 of 10 students are black or Hispanic — from fewer than 34 percent in 1991–92.

Among Latino students, 76 percent were in predominantly minority schools in 1998–99, from 73 percent in 1991–92, and 37 percent were in intensely minority schools, from 34 percent.

In a regional breakdown, the report found that minorities were most likely to attend school with whites in the South, although it was also in the South that integration was unraveling most quickly. The share of black students in predominantly white schools there dropped to 33 percent from 44 percent in the seven years ended 1998–99.

By two measures — of all black students, the percentage in majority-white schools; and of all white students, the percentage in schools attended by statistically typical black students — the report found schools in New York State to be the most segregated in the nation, followed by those in Michigan, Illinois and California. By the third measure the study examined to discern differences among states — the percentage of blacks in intensely minority schools — New York's schools were the third-most-segregated.

The report said the national trend "is contributing to a growing gap in quality between the schools being attended by white students and those serving a large proportion of minority students." It said that "racial differences in achievement and graduation began to expand in the 1990's, after having closed substantially from the 1960's to the mid-1980's," a period of generally steady desegregation.

A map of schools attended by the average black or Hispanic student would almost perfectly match a map of high-poverty schools, said the study's principal author, Gary Orfield, co-director of Harvard's Civil Rights Project. These poorer schools, the report said, have more transient student bodies, fewer teachers qualified in their subject areas, parents lacking political power, more frequent health problems among students and lower test scores.

Conservatives argue that in explaining school performance, the study places too much emphasis on racial breakdown, and that the way to close the gap between whites and minorities has less to do with integration than with raising academic standards for all.

But Professor Orfield said he believed that efforts by the White House and Congress to toughen school accountability through annual testing would probably backfire, driving minority children in failing schools to repeat grades and eventually drop out.

The report was the latest of a series since the 1970's in which Professor Orfield and various colleagues have monitored efforts to desegregate the schools.

Sept. 11 Attack Narrows the Racial Divide

BY SOMINI SENGUPTA | OCT. 10, 2001

IN FORT GREENE, Brooklyn, a crew of black and Latino teenage boys say they can no longer think of the police as enemies. Since Sept. 11, the boys say, the officers who patrol their neighborhoods, most of whom are white, no longer eye them with suspicion.

Several Haitian-American groups, which had angrily protested police abuse in recent years, have sent a letter to a local police chief in Crown Heights expressing admiration for the officers.

Mayor Rudolph W. Giuliani has been embraced by black leaders. On the national stage, with few exceptions, black members of Congress, seething all year long about the election of George W. Bush, have rallied to his side.

Black New Yorkers joke among themselves about their own reprieve from racial profiling. Even the language of racial grievance has shifted: Overnight, the cries about driving while black have become flying while brown — a phrase referring to reports of Muslim-Americans being asked to get off planes.

Ever so slightly, the attacks on the trade center have tweaked the city's traditional racial divisions.

This is not unheard of in wartime, historians say. Nor do most people believe it will last long. The black-white racial pattern has too deep a history.

But the signs of change have revealed themselves in dozens of interviews across the city in recent weeks. Some of it is evident in how police and civilians see each other. Some of it is how ordinary men and women react to each other on the streets, on subways, in bodegas. Some people attribute it to the solemnity that hangs over the city, others to fear, still others to a newfound unity as Americans. Whatever it is, the way that New Yorkers perceive one another across color lines — however accurate those perceptions were to begin with — has changed.

If old racial antagonisms have dissolved, new anxieties have surfaced.

Keith Wright, an assemblyman from Harlem, said that before Sept. 11, "people were looking at young black men like they were all suspected of some kind of crime."

"Now people are looking at people of Middle Eastern descent as suspects of terrorism," said Mr. Wright, who is black. "Now we have to be careful not to do that."

The New York Police Department has seen a rash of possible hate crimes against Arabs, Muslims, Sikhs — in short, anyone perceived by untrained eyes to be suspect in the terrorist attack. Yemeni-owned delis have been vandalized, shopkeepers and newsstand workers have been punched, a Sikh cabdriver has been shot at, Arabs and Pakistanis have been attacked on subways and on the street. Of the 120 alleged bias incidents reported to the police since Sept. 11, 80 have been against Arabs and South Asians; the suspects are whites, blacks and Hispanics.

Late last month, a Star-Ledger/Eagleton-Rutgers poll taken in New Jersey asked whether airport officials should regard Middle Eastern travelers with "more suspicion" than others. Blacks and whites differed only slightly in their responses: 38 percent of blacks and 42 percent of whites said those travelers should be treated with more suspicion. On the question of whether immigration from the Middle East should be "more restrictive than it is now," the differences were similarly small: 29 percent of blacks and 23 percent of whites said such immigration should be halted, while 55 percent of blacks and 56 percent of whites said it should be limited.

At the center of the shift in attitude is the group of boys playing football on a balmy afternoon last week at Fort Greene Park. Some of them are African-Americans, others have roots in the Caribbean; the family of one fled war in El Salvador. "The police would probably racially profile everyone that's here," said Louis Johnson, 18, pointing to his friends with a jut of his chin.

The child of Trinidadian immigrants, Mr. Johnson said he had all but grown accustomed to being trailed by the police. "They used to watch me from the time they see me, they watch me till I leave," he said. "But now they don't really bother us. They, like, stop everyone that has Middle Eastern features. They stop them. They ask them questions like that."

The boys see themselves transformed. "I just thought of myself as black," Mr. Johnson said. "But now I feel like I'm an American, more than ever."

Miqueo Rawell-Peterson, 17, notes gravely that the police were among the first to rush into the burning towers. "We've become a little more at ease with the policemen," he said. "We realize what they've done. Now we look at them more as heroes, instead of — I guess, what you'd say, enemies."

Police on the street call this going "from zero to hero" as people smile and say thank you and call in with tips. "Everyone's taken a second look at how they conduct themselves," said Lt. James Woods, a community relations officer at the Brooklyn South patrol office. "There's a lot more public display of affection, of support, of kindness."

Sgt. Thomas Seyfarth was stationed at a subway platform in central Brooklyn recently when a call came over the police radio about a man, apparently of Middle Eastern descent, sitting on a bench on a subway platform, but not taking a train. "Nobody ever would have called that in before," Sergeant Seyfarth said. (As it turned out, the man was on the wrong platform, waiting for a train going in the opposite direction.)

"I guess it's in fashion now," Sergeant Seyfarth said, referring to the new spirit of cooperation. "It's different. It's something you're not used to."

"Can't get too used to it, though," he added quickly. "The people who don't like you will be vocal again."

The examples offered as evidence of change are mundane

encounters — the way someone talks to you, a look on a stranger's face. Always, they are matters of perception.

Richard Greene, director of the Crown Heights Youth Collective, recalled an open-air memorial held in front of the home of a victim of the attack on the trade center. At the sight of some police officers, one young black man, Mr. Greene recalled, groused: "What are they doing here?" A second man, whom Mr. Greene overheard, explained that the police were there to keep traffic off the block. "It neutralized it right away," Mr. Greene said.

It may not have happened the same way before Sept. 11. "Absolutely, it has altered human relations," Mr. Greene surmised. "Race has a piece in that. Everyone in New York has had a sobering wake-up call as to our frailty as human beings."

To Joyce Hata, an Asian-American living in largely African-American Fort Greene, that call has given people permission to talk across the usual racial divides. Ms. Hata said she is used to being on the receiving end of cold stares from some of her neighbors. But the other day, she found herself in an unusually candid conversation with a middle-aged black woman on the street; the woman, Ms. Hata learned, she had just lost three of her neighbors.

"She's someone who would have been less accessible," Ms. Hata, 38, observed last Sunday after services at the Lafayette Avenue Presbyterian Church. "It's easier to break through now. People are so desperate to have someone hear them."

If people are talking, what they are talking about has changed, too, the pastor of that church, the Rev. David Dyson, noted. Mr. Dyson, who is white, said that people at the bodega down the street now ask each other: "How are you? How's the church? How's the family?"

"I haven't heard the word gentrification uttered since this happened," Mr. Dyson said. "There's not nearly as much us against them — the old us against them."

In Greenpoint, Brooklyn, Victor Lavalle, a writer, paints two pictures. The first is of his local pizzeria. Before Sept. 11, it was the usual

New York jostling: the mostly black and Latino boys from the neighborhood high school would come in, loud and rambunctious, prompting dirty looks from the elderly Polish women. After Sept. 11, the boys come in quietly. They ask the women if they've ordered. The women look at them, step aside and say, "Go ahead."

The second picture he paints is of an Indian-American friend. Last week, the friend started to park his car on a residential street in New Jersey, only to be greeted by a volley of threats and insults from a white man who stepped out of his house. Mr. Lavalle said his friend got back in his car and drove away, chilled to the bone.

Obama Elected President as Racial Barrier Falls

BY ADAM NAGOURNEY | NOV. 4, 2008

BARACK HUSSEIN OBAMA was elected the 44th president of the United States on Tuesday, sweeping away the last racial barrier in American politics with ease as the country chose him as its first black chief executive.

The election of Mr. Obama amounted to a national catharsis — a repudiation of a historically unpopular Republican president and his economic and foreign policies, and an embrace of Mr. Obama's call for a change in the direction and the tone of the country.

But it was just as much a strikingly symbolic moment in the evolution of the nation's fraught racial history, a breakthrough that would have seemed unthinkable just two years ago.

Mr. Obama, 47, a first-term senator from Illinois, defeated Senator John McCain of Arizona, 72, a former prisoner of war who was making his second bid for the presidency.

To the very end, Mr. McCain's campaign was eclipsed by an opponent who was nothing short of a phenomenon, drawing huge crowds epitomized by the tens of thousands of people who turned out to hear Mr. Obama's victory speech in Grant Park in Chicago.

Mr. McCain also fought the headwinds of a relentlessly hostile political environment, weighted down with the baggage left to him by President Bush and an economic collapse that took place in the middle of the general election campaign.

"If there is anyone out there who still doubts that America is a place where all things are possible, who still wonders if the dream of our founders is alive in our time, who still questions the power of our democracy, tonight is your answer," said Mr. Obama, standing before a huge wooden lectern with a row of American flags at his back, casting his eyes to a crowd that stretched far into the Chicago night.

"It's been a long time coming," the president-elect added, "but

President-elect Barack Obama with his wife, Michelle, and Vice President-elect Joseph R. Biden Jr. with his wife, Jill, in Chicago.

tonight, because of what we did on this date in this election at this defining moment, change has come to America."

Mr. McCain delivered his concession speech under clear skies on the lush lawn of the Arizona Biltmore, in Phoenix, where he and his wife had held their wedding reception. The crowd reacted with scattered boos as he offered his congratulations to Mr. Obama and saluted the historical significance of the moment.

"This is a historic election, and I recognize the significance it has for African-Americans and for the special pride that must be theirs tonight," Mr. McCain said, adding, "We both realize that we have come a long way from the injustices that once stained our nation's reputation."

Not only did Mr. Obama capture the presidency, but he led his party to sharp gains in Congress. This puts Democrats in control of the House, the Senate and the White House for the first time since 1995, when Bill Clinton was in office.

The day shimmered with history as voters began lining up before dawn, hours before polls opened, to take part in the culmination of a campaign that over the course of two years commanded an extraordinary amount of attention from the American public.

As the returns became known, and Mr. Obama passed milestone after milestone — Ohio, Florida, Virginia, Pennsylvania, New Hampshire, Iowa and New Mexico — people rolled spontaneously into the streets to celebrate what many described, with perhaps overstated if understandable exhilaration, a new era in a country where just 143 years ago, Mr. Obama, as a black man, could have been owned as a slave.

For Republicans, especially the conservatives who have dominated the party for nearly three decades, the night represented a bitter setback and left them contemplating where they now stand in American politics.

Mr. Obama and his expanded Democratic majority on Capitol Hill now face the task of governing the country through a difficult period: the likelihood of a deep and prolonged recession, and two wars. He took note of those circumstances in a speech that was notable for its sobriety and its absence of the triumphalism that he might understandably have displayed on a night when he won an Electoral College landslide.

"The road ahead will be long, our climb will be steep," said Mr. Obama, his audience hushed and attentive, with some, including the Rev. Jesse Jackson, wiping tears from their eyes. "We may not get there in one year or even one term, but America, I have never been more hopeful than I am tonight that we will get there. I promise you, we as a people will get there." The roster of defeated Republicans included some notable party moderates, like Senator John E. Sununu of New Hampshire and Representative Christopher Shays of Connecticut, and signaled that the Republican conference convening early next year in Washington will be not only smaller but more conservative.

Mr. Obama will come into office after an election in which he laid out a number of clear promises: to cut taxes for most Americans, to get the United States out of Iraq in a fast and orderly fashion, and to expand health care.

In a recognition of the difficult transition he faces, given the economic crisis, Mr. Obama is expected to begin filling White House jobs as early as this week.

Mr. Obama defeated Mr. McCain in Ohio, a central battleground in American politics, despite a huge effort that brought Mr. McCain and his running mate, Gov. Sarah Palin of Alaska, back there repeatedly. Mr. Obama had lost the state decisively to Senator Hillary Rodham Clinton of New York in the Democratic primary.

Mr. McCain failed to take from Mr. Obama the two Democratic states that were at the top of his target list: New Hampshire and Pennsylvania. Mr. Obama also held on to Minnesota, the state that played host to the convention that nominated Mr. McCain; Wisconsin; and Michigan, a state Mr. McCain once had in his sights.

The apparent breadth of Mr. Obama's sweep left Republicans sobered, and his showing in states like Ohio and Pennsylvania stood out because officials in both parties had said that his struggles there in the primary campaign reflected the resistance of blue-collar voters to supporting a black candidate.

"I always thought there was a potential prejudice factor in the state," Senator Bob Casey, a Democrat of Pennsylvania who was an early Obama supporter, told reporters in Chicago. "I hope this means we washed that away."

Mr. McCain called Mr. Obama at 10 p.m., Central time, to offer his congratulations. In the call, Mr. Obama said he was eager to sit down and talk; in his concession speech, Mr. McCain said he was ready to help Mr. Obama work through difficult times.

"I need your help," Mr. Obama told his rival, according to an Obama adviser, Robert Gibbs. "You're a leader on so many important issues."

Mr. Bush called Mr. Obama shortly after 10 p.m. to congratulate him on his victory.

"I promise to make this a smooth transition," the president said to Mr. Obama, according to a transcript provided by the White House. "You are about to go on one of the great journeys of life.

Congratulations, and go enjoy yourself."

For most Americans, the news of Mr. Obama's election came at 11 p.m., Eastern time, when the networks, waiting for the close of polls in California, declared him the victor. A roar sounded from the 125,000 people gathered in Hutchison Field in Grant Park at the moment that they learned Mr. Obama had been projected the winner.

The scene in Phoenix was decidedly more sour. At several points, Mr. McCain, unsmiling, had to motion his crowd to quiet down — he held out both hands, palms down — when they responded to his words of tribute to Mr. Obama with boos.

Mr. Obama, who watched Mr. McCain's speech from his hotel room in Chicago, offered a hand to voters who had not supported him in this election, when he took the stage 15 minutes later. "To those Americans whose support I have yet to earn,"he said, "I may not have won your vote, but I hear your voices, I need your help, and I will be your president, too."

Initial signs were that Mr. Obama benefited from a huge turnout of voters, but particularly among blacks. That group made up 13 percent of the electorate, according to surveys of people leaving the polls, compared with 11 percent in 2006.

In North Carolina, Republicans said that the huge surge of African-Americans was one of the big factors that led to Senator Elizabeth Dole, a Republican, losing her re-election bid.

Mr. Obama also did strikingly well among Hispanic voters; Mr. McCain did worse among those voters than Mr. Bush did in 2004. That suggests the damage the Republican Party has suffered among those voters over four years in which Republicans have been at the forefront on the effort to crack down on illegal immigrants.

The election ended what by any definition was one of the most remarkable contests in American political history, drawing what was by every appearance unparalleled public interest.

Throughout the day, people lined up at the polls for hours — some showing up before dawn — to cast their votes. Aides to both campaigns said that anecdotal evidence suggested record-high voter turnout.

Reflecting the intensity of the two candidates, Mr. McCain and Mr. Obama took a page from what Mr. Bush did in 2004 and continued to campaign after the polls opened.

Mr. McCain left his home in Arizona after voting early Tuesday to fly to Colorado and New Mexico, two states where Mr. Bush won four years ago but where Mr. Obama waged a spirited battle.

These were symbolically appropriate final campaign stops for Mr. McCain, reflecting the imperative he felt of trying to defend Republican states against a challenge from Mr. Obama.

"Get out there and vote," Mr. McCain said in Grand Junction, Colo. "I need your help. Volunteer, knock on doors, get your neighbors to the polls, drag them there if you need to."

By contrast, Mr. Obama flew from his home in Chicago to Indiana, a state that in many ways came to epitomize the audacity of his effort this year. Indiana has not voted for a Democrat since President Lyndon B. Johnson's landslide victory in 1964, and Mr. Obama made an intense bid for support there. He later returned home to Chicago to play basketball, his election-day ritual.

ELISABETH BUMILLER CONTRIBUTED REPORTING FROM PHOENIX, MARJORIE CONNELLY FROM NEW YORK AND JEFF ZELENY FROM CHICAGO.

A Lynching in Brooklyn

OPINION | BY THE NEW YORK TIMES | DEC. 16, 2008

THE MURDER OF José Sucuzhañay, an Ecuadorean immigrant who died over the weekend at a hospital in Queens, has thrown a harsh light onto a savage, hate-inspired crime that should sicken us all. This horror is also a reminder that bigotry can be deadly, not just to the groups intentionally targeted, but to anyone unfortunate enough to cross its path.

José and his brother Romel appear to have been misidentified as gay as they walked home, arms around each other, on a predawn morning in the Bushwick section of Brooklyn. Romel managed to escape the three men who emerged from a passing car wielding a baseball bat and shouting anti-gay and anti-Latino epithets.

José was struck on the head with a bottle, then kicked and beaten into unconsciousness. He was subsequently declared brain dead and expired last Friday night, one day before his mother, who was traveling from Ecuador, could reach him.

The victim, who had come to this country a decade ago, had been living the immigrant dream. Starting out as a waiter, he eventually bought several buildings and became co-owner of a real estate agency in Bushwick. He cared for his community and was well-liked in return.

This was the second recent killing of an Ecuadorean in the New York area. In November, Marcelo Lucero was stabbed and beaten in the Long Island village of Patchogue by a group of teenagers who, the police say, had been roaming the streets looking to beat up "a Mexican."

Several teenagers have been arrested and charged in the Long Island case. But New York City police, who are still searching for Mr. Sucuzhañay's killers, need to do all they can to bring those people to justice. A lynching in the heart of New York City is more than enough to remind us that bigotry cannot be tolerated.

For Puerto Ricans, Sotomayor's Success Stirs Pride

BY DAVID GONZALEZ | AUG. 6, 2009

IN THE SUMMER of 1959, Edwin Torres landed a $60-a-week job and wound up on the front page of El Diario. He had just been hired as the first Puerto Rican assistant district attorney in New York — and probably, he thinks, the entire United States.

He still recalls the headline: "Exemplary Son of El Barrio Becomes Prosecutor."

"You would've thought I had been named attorney general," he said. "That's how big it was."

Half a century later, the long and sometimes bittersweet history of Puerto Ricans in New York added a celebratory chapter on Thursday as the Senate confirmed Judge Sonia Sotomayor's nomination to the Supreme Court. Her personal journey — from a single-parent home in the Bronx projects to the Ivy League and an impressive legal career — has provoked a fierce pride in many other Puerto Ricans who glimpse reflections of their own struggles.

"This is about the acceptance that eluded us," said Mr. Torres, 78, who himself earned distinction as a jurist, novelist and raconteur. "It is beyond anybody's imagination when I started that a Puerto Rican could ascend to that position, to the Supreme Court."

Arguably the highest rung that any Puerto Rican has yet reached in this country, the confirmation of Judge Sotomayor is a watershed event for Puerto Rican New York. It builds on the achievements that others of her generation have made in business, politics, the arts and pop culture. It extends the legacy of an earlier, lesser-known generation who created social service and educational institutions that persist today, helping newcomers from Mexico and the Dominican Republic.

Yet the city has also been a place of heartbreak. Though Puerto Ricans were granted citizenship in 1917 and large numbers of them arrived in New York in the 1950s, poverty and lack of opportunity still pockmark some of their neighborhoods. A 2004 report by a Hispanic advocacy group showed that compared with other Latino groups nationwide, Puerto Ricans had the highest poverty rate, the lowest average family income and the highest unemployment rate for men.

In politics, the trailblazer Herman Badillo saw his career go from a series of heady firsts in the 1960s to frustration in the 1980s when his dreams of becoming the city's first Puerto Rican mayor were foiled by Harlem's political bosses. Just four years ago, Fernando Ferrer was trounced in his bid against Mayor Michael R. Bloomberg.

All those setbacks lose their sting, if only for a moment, in the glow of Judge Sotomayor's achievement, which many of her fellow Puerto Ricans say is as monumental for them as President Obama's election was for African-Americans. It has affirmed a sense of Puerto Rican identity at a moment when that distinction is often obscured by catch-all labels like Latino and Hispanic — and even as it is subjected to negative comparisons.

"Many elite Latin Americans have implied that Puerto Ricans blew it, because we had citizenship and did nothing," said Lillian Jimenez, a documentary filmmaker who co-produced a series of television ads in support of Judge Sotomayor's nomination. "But we were the biggest Spanish-speaking group in New York for decades, and bore the brunt of discrimination, especially in the 1950s. We struggled for our rights. We have people everywhere doing all kinds of things. But that history has not been known."

That history is in danger of disappearing in East Harlem, long the cradle of Puerto Rican New York. After waves of gentrification and development, parts of the area are now being advertised as Upper Yorkville, a new annex to the predominantly white Upper East Side. While the poor have stayed behind, many of East Harlem's successful sons and daughters have scattered to the suburbs.

"We have a whole intellectual and professional class that is invisible — people who came up through the neighborhood, with a working-class background, who really excelled," said Angelo Falcon, president of the National Institute for Latino Policy.

"But it's so dispersed, people don't see it. They do not make up a real, physical community, but they have the identity."

For those who paved the way for Judge Sotomayor, embracing that identity was the first step in charting their personal and professional paths out of hardship. Manuel del Valle, 60, an overachiever from the housing projects on Amsterdam Avenue, made the same leaps as the judge — to Princeton University and Yale Law School — but preceded her by five years.

Taking a cue from the black students at Princeton, he and the handful of other working-class Puerto Ricans from New York pressured university officials to offer a course on Puerto Rican history and to admit more minority students. They saw their goal as creating a class of lawyers, doctors, writers and activists who would use their expertise to lift up their old neighborhoods.

"Talk about arrogance," said Mr. del Valle, who now teaches law in Puerto Rico. "We actually believed we would have a dynamic impact on all the institutions American society had to offer."

"We were invisible," he said. "She made us visible."

In New York, many have welcomed the judge's visibility during a summer when the most celebrated — and reviled — local politicians were two Puerto Rican state senators who brought the state government to a standstill by mounting an abortive coup against their fellow Democrats.

"She really came at a moment when there is a public reassessment of the value of identity politics through this brouhaha in the Senate," said Arlene Davila, a professor of anthropology at New York University who has written extensively on Puerto Rican and Latino identity. "Here came this woman who reinvigorated us with the idea that a Latina can have a lot to contribute, not just to their own group, but to the entire American society."

But it is among her own — in the South Bronx, East Harlem or the Los Sures neighborhood of Brooklyn — where Judge Sotomayor's success resonates loudest, for the simple reason that many people understand the level of perseverance she needed to achieve it.

Orlando Plaza, 41, who took time off from his doctoral studies in history about five years ago to open Camaradas, a popular bar in East Harlem, sees her appeal as a sort of ethnic Rorschach test.

"Whether it's growing up in the Bronx, going to Catholic school or being from a single-parent household, there are so many tropes in her own story that we feel pride that someone from a background like ours achieved something so enormous," he said. "This is the real Jenny from the block."

And it is on the block, among the men and women who left Puerto Rico decades ago so their children might one day become professionals, where her story is most sweetly savored. The faces of the men and women playing dominoes or shooting pool at the Betances Senior Center in the Bronx attest to decades of hard work.

Many of them came to New York as teenagers more out of despair than dreams. Lucy Medina, who arrived in the 1950s, worked as a keypunch operator and in other jobs as she single-handedly raised two children. Today, her son is a captain in the city's Department of Correction and her daughter is a real estate executive.

Impressive as the judge's accomplishments are, Ms. Medina is more impressed with the judge's mother, Celina Sotomayor, who did what she had to do in order to raise two successful children in the projects.

"Her mother and I are very similar," said Ms. Medina, 77. "I know what she went through. We sacrificed ourselves so our children would get an education and get ahead. A lot of women here have done that. We stayed on top of our children and made sure they didn't get sidetracked."

Deep Tensions Rise to Surface After Ferguson Shooting

BY TANZINA VEGA AND JOHN ELIGON | AUG. 16, 2014

FERGUSON, MO. — Garland Moore, a hospital worker, lived in this St. Louis suburb for much of his 33 years, a period in which a largely white community has become a largely black one.

He attended its schools and is raising his family in this place of suburban homes and apartment buildings on the outskirts of a struggling Midwest city. And over time, he has felt his life to be circumscribed by Ferguson's demographics.

Mr. Moore, who is black, talks of how he has felt the wrath of the police here and in surrounding suburbs for years — roughed up during a minor traffic stop and prevented from entering a park when he was wearing St. Louis Cardinals red.

And last week, as he stood at a vigil for an unarmed 18-year-old shot dead by the police — a shooting that provoked renewed street violence and looting early Saturday — Mr. Moore heard anger welling and listened to a shout of: "We're tired of the racist police department."

"It broke the camel's back," Mr. Moore said of the killing of the teenager, Michael Brown. Referring to the northern part of St. Louis County, he continued, "The people in North County — not just African-Americans, some of the white people, too — they are tired of the police

The origins of the area's complex social and racial history date to the 19th century when the city of St. Louis and St. Louis County went their separate ways, leading to the formation of dozens of smaller communities outside St. Louis. Missouri itself has always been a state with roots in both the Midwest and the South, and racial issues intensified in the 20th century as St. Louis became a stopping point for the northern migration of Southern blacks seeking factory jobs in Detroit and Chicago.

As African-Americans moved into the city and whites moved out, real estate agents and city leaders, in a pattern familiar elsewhere in

Protesters angered over the police shooting of Michael Brown, 18, squared off with law enforcement in the streets of Ferguson, Mo.

the country, conspired to keep blacks out of the suburbs through the use of zoning ordinances and restrictive covenants. But by the 1970s, some of those barriers had started to fall, and whites moved even farther away from the city. These days, Ferguson is like many of the suburbs around St. Louis, inner-ring towns that accommodated white flight decades ago but that are now largely black. And yet they retain a white power structure.

Although about two-thirds of Ferguson residents are black, its mayor and five of its six City Council members are white. Only three of the town's 53 police officers are black.

Turnout for local elections in Ferguson has been poor. The mayor, James W. Knowles III, noted his disappointment with the turnout — about 12 percent — in the most recent mayoral election during a City Council meeting in April. Patricia Bynes, a black woman who is the Democratic committeewoman for the Ferguson area, said the lack of black involvement in local government was partly the result of the black population's being more transient in small municipalities and less attached to them.

There is also some frustration among blacks who say town government is not attuned to their concerns.

Aliyah Woods, 45, once petitioned Ferguson officials for a sign that would warn drivers that a deaf family lived on that block. But the sign never came. "You get tired," she said. "You keep asking, you keep asking. Nothing gets done."

Mr. Moore, who recently moved to neighboring Florissant, said he had attended a couple of Ferguson Council meetings to complain that the police should be patrolling the residential streets to try to prevent break-ins rather than lying in wait to catch people for traffic violations.

This year, community members voiced anger after the all-white, seven-member school board for the Ferguson-Florissant district pushed aside its black superintendent for unrevealed reasons. That spurred several blacks to run for three board positions up for election, but only one won a seat.

The St. Louis County Police Department fired a white lieutenant last year for ordering officers to target blacks in shopping areas. That resulted in the department's enlisting researchers at the University of California, Los Angeles, to study whether the department was engaging in racial profiling.

And in recent years, two school districts in North County lost their accreditation. One, Normandy, where Mr. Brown graduated this year, serves parts of Ferguson. When parents in the mostly black district sought to allow their children to transfer to schools in mostly white districts, they said, they felt a backlash with racial undertones. Frustration with underfunded and underperforming schools has long been a problem, and when Gov. Jay Nixon held a news conference on Friday to discuss safety and security in Ferguson, he was confronted with angry residents demanding to know what he would do to fix their schools.

Ferguson's economic shortcomings reflect the struggles of much of the region. Its median household income of about $37,000 is less than the statewide number, and its poverty level of 22 percent outpaces the state's by seven percentage points.

In Ferguson, residents say most racial tensions have to do with an overzealous police force.

"It is the people in a position of authority in our community that have to come forward," said Jerome Jenkins, 47, who, with his wife, Cathy, owns Cathy's Kitchen, a downtown Ferguson restaurant.

"What you are witnessing is our little small government has to conform to the change that we are trying to do," Mr. Jenkins added. "Sometimes things happen for a purpose; maybe we can get it right."

Ferguson's police chief, Thomas Jackson, has been working with the Justice Department's community relations team on improving interaction with residents. At a news conference here last week, he acknowledged some of the problems.

"I've been trying to increase the diversity of the department ever since I got here," Chief Jackson said, adding that "race relations is a top priority right now." As for working the with Justice Department, he said, "I told them, 'Tell me what to do, and I'll do it.'"

Although experience and statistics suggest that Ferguson's police force disproportionately targets blacks, it is not as imbalanced as in some neighboring departments in St. Louis County. While blacks are 37 percent more likely to be pulled over compared with their proportion of the population in Ferguson, that is less than the statewide average of 59 percent, according to Richard Rosenfeld, a professor of criminology at the University of Missouri-St. Louis.

In fact, Mr. Rosenfeld said, Ferguson did not fit the profile of a community that would be a spark for civil unrest. The town has "pockets of disadvantage" and middle and upper-middle income families. He said Ferguson had benefited in the last five to 10 years from economic growth in the northern part of the county, such as the expansion of Express Scripts, the Fortune 500 health care giant.

"Ferguson does not stand out as the type of community where you would expect tensions with the police to boil over into violence and looting," Mr. Rosenfeld said.

But the memory of the region's racial history lingers.

In 1949, a mob of whites showed up to attack blacks who lined up to get into the pool at Fairground Park in north St. Louis after it had been desegregated.

In the 1970s, a court battle over public school inequality led to a settlement that created a desegregation busing program that exists to this day.

A Ferguson city councilman caused a stir in 1970 when he used racially charged language to criticize teenagers from the neighboring town of Kinloch for throwing rocks and bottles at homes in Ferguson. The councilman, Carl Kersting, said, "We should call a black a black, and not be afraid to face up to these people," according to an article in the St. Louis Globe-Democrat.

Eventually blacks broke down the barriers in the inner ring of suburbs, and whites fled farther out. But whites fought hard to protect their turf.

In the mid-1970s, Alyce Herndon, a black woman, moved with her family to what was then the mostly white town of Jennings in St. Louis County. She said some of their white neighbors stuck an Afro pick in their front lawn and set it on fire. Ms. Herndon also recalled tensions flaring between black and white students at her school after the television mini-series "Roots" first aired in 1977.

For all its segregation and discrimination, St. Louis did not have the major riots and unrest during the 1960s that was seen across the country.

St. Louis's black leaders "were able to pressure businesses and schools to open their doors to black people and employers to hire black workers," Stefan Bradley, the director of African-American studies at St. Louis University, wrote in an email. "These concessions may have been enough to prevent St. Louis from taking what many believed to be the next step toward redress of injustice: violent rebellion."

But the fatal shooting of Mr. Brown has brought submerged tensions to the surface.

"St. Louis never has had its true race moment, where they had to confront this," said Ms. Bynes, the Democratic committeewoman. Without that moment, she added, blacks have been complacent when it comes to local politics. "I'm hoping that this is what it takes to get the pendulum to swing the other way."

Ms. Herndon, 49, said she moved her family to Ferguson in 2003 because she felt it was a good community, safer than the unincorporated portion of the county where they lived previously and with better schools for her children.

The town, she said, offers everything — places to shop, eat and drink. There is a farmers market on Saturdays. She frequents a wine bar across from a lot where a band plays on Fridays. She has white and Asian neighbors on either side of her, and there are other black families on her block. She has not experienced the racial tensions of her childhood in St. Louis County, she said, but she understands that the younger generation is living a different experience than she is.

"I understand the anger because it's psychological trauma when you see so many people being shot or people being falsely accused," said Ms. Herndon, who over the past week has avoided the streets that have been filled with tear gas and rubber bullets in clashes between police and protesters.

But now, a population of young black men who often feel forgotten actually feel that people are finally listening.

"If it wasn't for the looting," said one man, who declined to give his name, "we wouldn't get the attention."

Mr. Moore went one step further. He does not condone the violence that erupted during some of the protests, he said, but he does understand the frustration. And if he were younger, he said, he probably would have joined them.

TANZINA VEGA REPORTED FROM FERGUSON, AND JOHN ELIGON FROM KANSAS CITY, MO. SERGE F. KOVALESKI CONTRIBUTED REPORTING FROM NEW YORK, AND JOHN SCHWARTZ FROM FERGUSON. ALAIN DELAQUÉRIÈRE CONTRIBUTED RESEARCH.

When Will Black Lives Matter in St. Louis?

OPINION | BY NICOLE D. NELSON | SEPT. 20, 2017

ST. LOUIS — On Aug. 9, 2014, Mike Brown was killed by Darren Wilson, a police officer in the St. Louis suburb Ferguson, Mo. What followed were months of overwhelmingly nonviolent protests that were policed by law enforcement officers who wore riot gear, shook their batons at protesters and took joy-rides in heavily armored military vehicles. In November 2014, a grand jury decided not to indict Mr. Wilson, and a few months later federal investigators cleared him of any wrongdoing.

Three years later, change the names to Anthony Lamar Smith and Jason Stockley, and here we are again.

On Friday, a former St. Louis police officer named Jason Stockley was acquitted of first-degree murder in the 2011 shooting death of Anthony Lamar Smith, 24, after a high-speed chase.

Just before he shot him, Mr. Stockley, who is white, told his partner he was "going to kill"him. In his decision in the bench trial, Judge Timothy Wilson of the St. Louis Circuit justified Mr. Stockley's remark by writing that people "say all kinds of things in the heat of the moment."

Prosecutors had also suggested that Mr. Stockley planted a gun in Mr. Smith's car after the chase ended, because the weapon contained his DNA, not Mr. Smith's. But Judge Wilson, who has nearly 30 years of experience, expressed doubts about this, noting that "an urban heroin dealer not in possession of a firearm would be an anomaly."

Welcome to St. Louis.

Not only are the local court system and law enforcement community committed to reinforcing that black lives do not matter here, but the police also continue to escalate tensions and foment distrust between them and protesters.

Around noon on Friday, my colleagues and I, along with other protesters, were marching peacefully through the streets of downtown

St. Louis when we saw the police department bringing in hundreds of officers in riot gear. In an ostentatious show of force, they lined up along the street to face us, holding their shields and batons aloft so protesters could clearly see them.

To say that these actions were unnecessary and exaggerated would be an understatement. They were clearly intended to make protesters fearful and to provoke unrest.

Demonstrations continued over the weekend and more than 80 people were arrested. By Sunday night, as I and other lawyers and advocates worked to bail out protesters, stories were flooding in about the unscrupulous methods officers were using to engage protesters and ultimately arrest them. Officers had shot rubber bullets into crowds of people, hitting pedestrians and innocent bystanders. Some who took off running to escape the onslaught of rubber bullets were chased and tackled by officers. Videos have since surfaced all over social media that substantiate protesters' accounts of police in riot gear cornering protesters and refusing to let them leave and go home, which resulted in numerous arrests.

As if this weren't problematic enough, St. Louis police officers were heard chanting, "Whose Streets? Our Streets!" This is a vile appropriation of a familiar chant that courageous demonstrators used in Ferguson. Can you imagine hearing police officers say those words as they advance on a crowd of protesters?

That sentiment isn't out of place in the St. Louis police department: Top brass echo it as well. At a news conference, Lawrence O'Toole, the acting police commissioner for the city of St. Louis, proclaimed that "police owned tonight." This is the kind of "leadership" that forces people of color and poor people into survival mode in this region.

In addition, our local officials lament the property damage that has occurred here, but not the grievances of the black community. On a Twitter post, Mayor Lyda Krewson labeled protesters alleged to have committed property damage downtown as "criminals." Her and Mr. O'Toole's willingness to speak out so emphatically against people who break windows, but not against police officers who kill citizens, is enraging for those of us in the black community and for our allies.

These protests are about so much more than Jason Stockley. They are about the many other Jason Stockleys in the St. Louis metropolitan and county police departments, and the city's refusal to acknowledge the pain that remains in this community before and since Aug. 9, 2014

These protests are about the continued predatory practices of the municipal court system here, which bleeds people dry in fines and fees. Some of our clients have taken out payday loans and borrowed against life insurance policies to pay such fines. Just last year, Arch-City Defenders reached a $4.75 million settlement in a debtors' prison class action lawsuit against the city of Jennings, which borders Ferguson, for illegally jailing people who were unable to pay traffic tickets or minor ordinance violations.

All of this is exhausting. The insensitivity. The mockery of real struggle and pain. The disregard. The arrogance.

When will Black Lives Matter in St. Louis? Which local leaders will finally step up and stop the government from continuing its long, complicated and devastating history of racism? From our view, military tanks, tear gas, rubber bullets and dishonest narratives won't be bridging this gap anytime soon.

The Ferguson Commission and the Movement for Black Lives, a collective of more than 50 organizations representing black Americans, have outlined a number of policy recommendations that would positively affect the black community and poor people: end cash bail, demilitarize law enforcement and stop criminalizing poverty. St. Louis officials must take these demands seriously and be willing to implement them.

Until then, St. Louis law enforcement officials will continue to find themselves locked in this pattern, wondering why black citizens take to the streets demanding that the police stop killing us.

NICOLE D. NELSON IS A STAFF ATTORNEY WITH ARCHCITY DEFENDERS.

The Heartbeat of Racism Is Denial

OPINION | BY IBRAM X. KENDI | JAN. 13, 2018

WHEN OUR REALITY is too ugly, we deny reality. It is too painful to look at. Reality is too hard to accept.

Mental health experts routinely say that denial is among the most common defense mechanisms. Denial is how the person defends his superior sense of self, her racially unequal society.

Denial is how America defends itself as superior to "shithole countries" in Africa and elsewhere, as President Trump reportedly described them in a White House meeting last week, although he has since, well, denied that. It's also how America defends itself as superior to those "developing countries" in Africa, to quote how liberal opponents of Mr. Trump might often describe them.

Mr. Trump appears to be unifying America — unifying Americans in their denial. The more racist Mr. Trump sounds, the more Trump country denies his racism, and the more his opponents look away from their own racism to brand Trump country as racist. Through it all, America remains a unified country of denial.

The reckoning of Mr. Trump's racism must become the reckoning of American racism. Because the American creed of denial — "I'm not a racist" — knows no political parties, no ideologies, no colors, no regions.

On Friday, Senator Richard J. Durbin, Democrat of Illinois, affirmed that Mr. Trump did use the term "shithole" during a White House meeting on immigration with lawmakers. Mr. Durbin rightfully described Mr. Trump's words as "hate-filled, vile and racist," and added, "I cannot believe that in the history of the White House in that Oval Office, any president has ever spoken the words that I personally heard our president speak yesterday."

But Mr. Trump is no exception. In framing Mr. Trump's racism as exceptional, in seeking to highlight the depth of the president's cruelty,

Mr. Durbin, a reliably liberal senator, showed the depth of denial of American racism.

Begin with the eight presidents who held slaves while in the Oval Office. Then consider how Abraham Lincoln urged black people to leave the United States. "Even when you cease to be slaves, you are yet far removed from being placed on an equality with the white race," Lincoln told five black guests at the White House in 1862. So "it is better for us both, therefore, to be separated."

Raging then as we are raging now, the abolitionist William Lloyd Garrison responded, "Can anything be more puerile, absurd, illogical, impertinent, untimely?" He added that "had it not been for the cupidity of their white enslavers, not one of their race would now be found upon this continent."

Presidential history also includes the social Darwinism of Theodore Roosevelt, the federal-government-segregating, "Birth of a Nation" — praising Woodrow Wilson — and the bigotry that came from the mouths of presidents who are generally seen as essential to racial progress. President Lyndon B. Johnson said "nigger" nearly as often as Ku Klux Klansmen did.

This denial of racism is the heartbeat of racism. Where there is suffering from racist policies, there are denials that those policies are racist. The beat of denial sounds the same across time and space.

I grew up to the beat of racist denial in Queens, not far from where Mr. Trump grew up. I was raised in the urban "hell" of neighborhoods he probably avoided, alongside immigrants from countries he derided last week. In school or elsewhere, we all heard recitals of the American ideal of equality, especially on the day we celebrate the life of the Rev. Dr. Martin Luther King Jr. Those events often feature recitals of the words "all men are created equal," which were written by a slaveholder who once declared that black people "are inferior to the whites in the endowments both of body and mind."

Thomas Jefferson was not a founding father of equality. He was a founding father of the heartbeat of denial that lives through both Mr.

Trump's denials and the assertion that his racial views are abnormal for America and its presidents.

Fifty years ago, Richard Nixon transformed this historic heartbeat of denial into an intoxicating political philosophy. His presidential candidacy appealed to George Wallace-type segregationists while also attracting Americans who refused to live near "dangerous" black residents, obstructed the desegregation of schools, resisted affirmative action policies, framed black mothers on welfare as undeserving, called the black family pathological and denigrated black culture — all those racists who refused to believe they were racist in 1968.

Nixon designed his campaign, one of his advisers explained, to allow a potential supporter to "avoid admitting to himself that he was attracted by" the "racist appeal."

A new vocabulary emerged, allowing users to evade admissions of racism. It still holds fast after all these years. The vocabulary list includes these: law and order. War on drugs. Model minority. Reverse discrimination. Race-neutral. Welfare queen. Handout. Tough on crime. Personal responsibility. Black-on-black crime. Achievement gap. No excuses. Race card. Colorblind. Post-racial. Illegal immigrant. Obamacare. War on Cops. Blue Lives Matter. All Lives Matter. Entitlements. Voter fraud. Economic anxiety.

The denials using these phrases come from both conservatives and white liberals who think people of color are stuck in cycles of unstable families and criminal cultures, and that the deprivations of poverty and discrimination spin out bad people.

Mr. Trump opened his candidacy with racism, calling Mexicans criminals and rapists. Since taking office, he has looked away from the disaster zone in Puerto Rico, he has called some violent white supremacists "very fine people," and he has described Nigerians as living in "huts."

When someone identifies the obvious, Mr. Trump resounds the beat of denial as he did before he was president: "I'm the least racist person that you've ever met," that "you've ever seen," that "you've ever encountered."

These are ugly denials. But it's the denials from those who stand in strong opposition to this president that are more frustrating to me: denials that their attacks on identity politics are racist. Denials that the paltry number of people of color in elite spaces marks racism.

Those denials echo the same ones that frustrated Dr. King in 1963 as he sat in a Birmingham jail cell and wrote, "Shallow understanding from people of good will is more frustrating than absolute misunderstanding from people of ill will."

Mr. Trump, I suspect, will go to his grave with his heart beating in denial of the ill will of racism. Many others will as well.

Because we naturally want to look away from our ugliness. We paint over racist reality to make a beautiful delusion of self, of society. We defend this beautiful self and society from our racist reality with the weapons of denial.

Denial is fueled by the stigma associated with being a racist. Feeding the stigma is how "racist" is considered almost like an identity, a brand.

But a racist is not who a person is. A racist is what a person is, what a person is saying, what a person is doing.

Racist is not a fixed category like "not racist," which is steeped denial. Only racists say they are not racist. Only the racist lives by the heartbeat of denial.

The antiracist lives by the opposite heartbeat, one that rarely and irregularly sounds in America — the heartbeat of confession.

IBRAM X. KENDI, A PROFESSOR OF HISTORY AND INTERNATIONAL RELATIONS AT AMERICAN UNIVERSITY, IS THE AUTHOR OF "STAMPED FROM THE BEGINNING: THE DEFINITIVE HISTORY OF RACIST IDEAS IN AMERICA."

There's Never Been a Native American Congresswoman. That Could Change in 2018.

BY JULIE TURKEWITZ | MARCH 19, 2018

ALBUQUERQUE — When Deb Haaland was a child, she would rise early on this state's sun-beaten tribal land, sling a water jar around her waist and climb the mesa overlooking her pueblo.

It was as high as she ever thought she would go.

Now, she is among a historic number of Native American women running for elective office. None has ever served in Congress, but that could change this year if Ms. Haaland wins.

In all, there are at least four indigenous women running for Congress, three more are bidding for governors' offices and another 31 are campaigning for seats in state legislatures — from both sides of the aisle.

The numbers far outstrip past election cycles, longtime observers of native politics say, and they are only partly driven by the liberal energy and #MeToo declarations that have flourished since President Trump's election.

More broadly, they are part of a decades-long shift in which native communities, long marginalized by United States voting laws and skeptical of a government that stripped them of land and traditions, are moving into mainstream politics.

Montana has more than a dozen Native Americans running for the state House this year. Utah tribes are pushing the governor to make a seat for them in his cabinet. Five native people serve in the Minnesota Legislature, and four of them are women.

"American Indians have been invisible for so long, in so many sectors in society," said Denise Juneau, who was among the first native women in the country to be elected to a statewide executive position

Deb Haaland, a Democratic candidate for Congress in New Mexico's First District, is one of six Native American women running for Congress or for governor this year, a marked increase from 2016.

when she became the Montana schools superintendent in 2009. In that role, she developed an Indian history curriculum that is being replicated across the American West. "To be able to make inroads in the political world," she said, "is huge."

Many of these candidates are running on a liberal platform fueled by opposition to the Trump administration, as Ms. Haaland is. But others are Republicans who don't fit that mold at all.

One is Andria Tupola, a Native Hawaiian lawmaker running for governor of Hawaii on a promise of tax cuts and small government. Another is Sharon Clahchischilliage, who was a co-chairwoman of Mr. Trump's Native American coalition in 2016 and is running for re-election to the New Mexico House on a platform she calls "fighting the environmentalists."

Ms. Clahchischilliage is a fierce advocate for a coal-fired power plant that employs many Navajo people. She is hoping Mr. Trump will halt the threatened closing of the plant. Keeping it open, she said, could save 1,600 jobs.

"What I love about Trump is that he understands," she said. "He gets it. He is asking: What regulations need to change?"

Here in Albuquerque, Ms. Haaland, a Democrat, recently won 35 percent of the vote in a six-candidate field at the state party convention. She is a "strong contender" to win the June primary, said Joe Monahan, a longtime New Mexico political blogger. (Her district covers most of Albuquerque and has elected Democrats for a decade).

"We're seeing a new generation of Native Americans who have seen more opportunity in education starting to knock down the doors in politics," Mr. Monahan said. "And it's not a loud movement, but it's a steady movement."

Ms. Haaland is a citizen of the Laguna Pueblo, a sovereign nation west of Albuquerque that is one of the country's 573 federally recognized tribes. A child of military veterans, she attended 13 public schools before graduating from high school, then started a salsa company and worked as a cake decorator before putting herself through college and law school on a mix of food stamps and student loans.

She entered politics in 2008 as a volunteer for Barack Obama, then spent years crisscrossing the state to register native voters in some of the country's most remote corners. In 2015, she became the head of the state Democratic Party and helped to flip the New Mexico House of Representatives back to Democratic control.

On the campaign trail, she frequently cites her heritage, and she makes the argument that many of the issues affecting native communities — the ubiquity of low-wage jobs, violence against women — afflict other groups as well.

"I know what it's like to get my health care from the Indian Health Service, and hold a sick child in the waiting room for three hours until you have a chance to see a doctor," she said in an interview at her headquarters, a sparsely furnished office downtown splashed with political signs saying "Healthcare Not Warfare" and "¡Obámanos Nuevo México!"

Her priority in Congress, she said, would be to turn New Mexico into a solar energy powerhouse, a message with appeal in an impoverished state that has struggled to diversify an economy dependent on oil and gas.

She faces a field crowded with qualified candidates, including Antoinette Sedillo Lopez, a former law school dean who has spent a career building social justice programs.

The main criticism of Ms. Haaland is that she is concealing a lack of policy depth by focusing on the historic nature of her candidacy. "That as a single theme could leave her vulnerable," Mr. Monahan said.

The United States did not grant native people full citizenship and the right to vote in federal elections until 1924, and for years they were mostly absent from federal government, according to Mark Trahant, a professor at the University of North Dakota who writes extensively about Native Americans in politics.

That began to change in the late 1950s, when Washington instituted a policy known as termination, abolishing tribal governments and taking Indian land.

Facing existential threats, native leaders began to exhort fellow Indians to vote and run for office. Men began to make elective inroads, and in recent years women have followed. In 2001, the coalition of tribes known as the National Congress of American Indians began a voting project that continues today.

To be sure, Native Americans are just 2 percent of the population, and low voter turnout persists in many communities.

But that is changing in some corners, and American Indians have the potential to sway elections in states like Montana, where they make up 7 percent of the voting-age population; New Mexico, where they are more than 10 percent; and Alaska, where they are more than 17 percent.

Today there are two native men in the United States House of Representatives, both Republicans from Oklahoma. (Elizabeth Warren, the senator from Massachusetts, has discussed having native heritage but is not enrolled in a tribe.)

Among the native women seeking office this year is Peggy Flanagan, a former director of a nonprofit organization who is running for lieutenant governor of Minnesota.

In an interview, Ms. Flanagan said that if she wins, she will oppose a proposed pipeline across historic Ojibwe land; send money meant to help native people to tribes rather than county governments; and bring attention to the country's many missing and murdered native women.

But Ms. Juneau, the Montana school superintendent, warned that the hardest part of winning an election as an Indian woman is proving that you can represent the entire state, not just its tribes.

"It's not like, as a person of color or as an American Indian woman, you can walk into a room and say: 'I'm qualified,' and everybody looks at you like that," she said. "You have to prove it. And we will — eventually.

Korematsu, Notorious Supreme Court Ruling on Japanese Internment, Is Finally Tossed Out

BY CHARLIE SAVAGE | JUNE 26, 2018

WASHINGTON — In the annals of Supreme Court history, a 1944 decision upholding the forcible internment of Japanese-Americans during World War II has long stood out as a stain that is almost universally recognized as a shameful mistake. Yet that notorious precedent, Korematsu v. United States, remained law because no case gave justices a good opportunity to overrule it.

But on Tuesday, when the Supreme Court's conservative majority upheld President Trump's ban on travel into the United States by citizens of several predominantly Muslim countries, Chief Justice John G. Roberts Jr. also seized the moment to finally overrule Korematsu.

"The forcible relocation of U.S. citizens to concentration camps, solely and explicitly on the basis of race, is objectively unlawful and outside the scope of presidential authority," he wrote. Citing language used by then-Justice Robert H. Jackson in a dissent to the 1944 ruling, Chief Justice Roberts added, "Korematsu was gravely wrong the day it was decided, has been overruled in the court of history, and — to be clear — 'has no place in law under the Constitution.' "

In a dissent of the travel ban ruling, Justice Sonia Sotomayor offered tepid applause. While the "formal repudiation of a shameful precedent is laudable and long overdue," she said, it failed to make the court's decision to uphold the travel ban acceptable or right. She accused the Justice Department and the court's majority of adopting troubling parallels between the two cases.

In both cases, she wrote, the court deferred to the Trump administration's invocation of "an ill-defined national security threat to justify an exclusionary policy of sweeping proportion," relying on stereotypes about a particular group amid "strong evidence that impermissible hostility and animus motivated the government's policy."

The fallacies in Korematsu were echoed in the travel ban ruling, warned Hiroshi Motomura, a University of California, Los Angeles, law professor who has written extensively about immigration.

"Overruling Korematsu the way the court did in this case reduces the overruling to symbolism that is so bare that it is deeply troubling, given the parts of the reasoning behind Korematsu that live on in today's decision: a willingness to paint with a broad brush by nationality, race or religion by claiming national security grounds," he said.

He added, "If the majority really wanted to bury Korematsu, they would have struck down the travel ban."

The Korematsu ruling, an exceedingly rare modern example in which the court explicitly upheld government discrimination against an entire category of people based upon a trait like race or ethnicity, traced back to the early days after Japan attacked Pearl Harbor and the United States entered World War II.

In 1942, President Franklin D. Roosevelt issued an executive order that permitted the military to exclude "any or all persons" from militarily sensitive areas to prevent espionage and sabotage, and to house them in internment camps. The military used that power to order all people of Japanese ancestry, including American citizens, removed from the West Coast.

Fred Korematsu, an American citizen living on the West Coast, refused to leave and was convicted of disobeying a military order. With help from the American Civil Liberties Union, he appealed the verdict to the Supreme Court. But the court voted, 6 to 3, to uphold the internment policy as a justified national security measure amid the wartime emergency.

Years later, as World War II receded and the civil rights movement unfolded, that policy — and the Supreme Court ruling upholding it — became widely seen as wrong. In 1982, a congressional commission called the policy a "grave injustice" that stemmed from "race prejudice, war hysteria and a failure of political leadership." In a concurrence, the government said "the decision in Korematsu lies overruled in the court of history."

In 1988, Congress passed a law, signed by President Ronald Reagan, providing $20,000 in reparations to each surviving detainee. A dozen years later, Justice Antonin Scalia invoked Korematsu as one of the most notorious mistakes of the court, alongside the Dred Scott decision, the pre-Civil War case denying freedom and citizenship to black slaves brought into free states.

A district court judge vacated Mr. Korematsu's conviction in 1984, citing in part the discovery that the Roosevelt-era Justice Department had misled the judiciary about the need for the policy, including by citing claims that Japanese-Americans were signaling offshore submarines that the executive branch had already decided were probably not true.

But because the government did not try again to detain entire categories of people in a protected class like race or religion, no case presented a good vehicle for the Supreme Court to overturn the precedent.

The travel ban case, however, brought Korematsu back to the forefront. It traced back to Mr. Trump's campaign proposal in 2015 to categorically bar Muslims from entering the United States. At the time, Mr. Trump cited with approval Roosevelt's actions, including wartime restrictions placed on Americans of Japanese, German and Italian ancestry, and said he was not going that far.

"Take a look at what F.D.R. did many years ago," Mr. Trump said at the time. "He did the same thing."

Over time, Mr. Trump's call for a complete ban on Muslims entering the United States evolved into a ban on entry by nationals from a list of troubled countries, most of which were predominantly Muslim. Under the law, the president has the authority to bar groups of foreigners for national security reasons.

The dispute before the Supreme Court was whether to block the government from carrying out a version of the ban that Mr. Trump issued in September. Even though that directive was neutral about religion, the history and context, like Mr. Trump's political rhetoric, suggested it was tainted by unconstitutional religious discrimination.

As the case unfolded, children of Japanese-Americans held in the detention camps and several public interest groups filed two supporting briefs urging the Supreme Court to see Mr. Trump's latest travel ban as essentially a new version of Roosevelt's order: demanding that the courts defer to the president's claimed national security judgments when he is, at least in effect, singling out an entire category of people based on a discriminatory animus.

But in his majority opinion, Chief Justice Roberts argued that Roosevelt's act had "nothing to do" with the travel ban case. The "morally repugnant order" that forced Japanese-American citizens from their West Coast homes and into detention camps "solely and explicitly on the basis of race" was different from "a facially neutral policy denying certain foreign nationals the privilege of admission" into the country, he wrote.

"The entry suspension is an act that is well within executive authority and could have been taken by any other president — the only question is evaluating the actions of this particular president in promulgating an otherwise valid proclamation," he wrote.

Justice Sotomayor, however, suggested that Chief Justice Roberts's majority decision in Trump v. Hawaii may go down in Supreme Court history as a second coming of Korematsu.

"By blindly accepting the government's misguided invitation to sanction a discriminatory policy motivated by animosity toward a disfavored group, all in the name of a superficial claim of national security, the court redeploys the same dangerous logic underlying Korematsu and merely replaces one 'gravely wrong' decision with another," she wrote.

Glossary

&c. Alternative form of "etc;" short for "et cetera," which is Latin for "and so forth."

abolitionist Person who wanted to end slavery.

Asiatic From or related to Asia.

boycott Form of protest involving large groups of people refusing to use a company or organization's goods or services.

bracero Spanish for "laborer."

caste System of dividing society into hierarchical classes.

civil rights The rights of each person in a society, including equality under the law, the right to vote and the right to equal employment opportunities and wages.

Democrat Member of the Democratic Party, the first political party in the United States. During the 19th century, the party supported slavery and opposed civil-rights reform. It underwent a monumental ideological shift in the early 20th century, at which point it began to support progressive reform, organized labor and civil rights, among other ideals.

desegregation The policy of ending separation by race.

Dred Scott v. Sanford Landmark decision by the United States Supreme Court in 1857 establishing that people of African descent were not and could not be American citizens.

Fifteenth Amendment Amendment to the United States Constitution establishing the right of all men, regardless of race or prior enslavement, to vote; ratified in February 1870.

fifth column Group of people who are perceived to be undermining a larger group from within, usually in favor of an enemy. Federal, state and city workers of Japanese descent were considered during World War II to be a fifth column.

Fourteenth Amendment Amendment to the United States Constitution granting citizenship, equal legal rights and equal civil rights to all people born or naturalized in the United States; ratified in July 1868.

Grecian bendback Also known as "Grecian bend," a style of skirt worn by women in the 1860s that caused them to lean forward.

industrial school Institution designed to teach students the skills necessary for a specific trade or job.

Jim Crow Caste system separating back people from white people in the United States, and relegating black people to the status of second-class citizens. The Jim Crow system and its laws were abolished by the Civil Rights Act of 1964.

Korematsu v. United States Landmark decision by the United States Supreme Court in 1944 that ordered Japanese-American citizens and non-citizens into internment camps during World War II.

Ku Klux Klan White supremacist hate group founded after the Civil War, resurrected in the early 20th century, and still in existence today.

left wing Liberal segment of a political party that supports social equality and fairness.

lynch To execute by mob someone accused of a crime without a legal trial, typically by hanging.

Loving v. Virgina Landmark decision by the United States Supreme Court in 1967 invalidating laws prohibiting interracial marriage.

Mason Dixon line Boundary between Maryland and Pennsylvania; considered the borderline between slave-owning and non slave-owning states prior to the abolition of slavery.

Niagara Movement Black civil-rights organization founded in 1905.

pannier A hooped petticoat worn under a skirt to expand the width of a woman's dress; worn in the 17th and 18 centuries.

Plessy v. Ferguson Landmark decision by the United States Supreme Court in 1896 upholding the constitutionality of "separate but equal;" the policy of racial segregation of public facilities provided both sets of facilities were of equal quality.

Radical Reconstruction Also known as Congressional Reconstruction, a post-Civil War initiative by Radical Republicans to provide black people with the same political rights and opportunities as white people through federal intervention.

Republican Member of the Republican Party, the forerunner of the modern Democratic Party that, in the 19th century, supported the abolition of slavery and institution of civil rights for minorities.

Scottsboro boys Legal case of nine young black men accused of raping two white women in 1931 in Scottsboro, Ala., the end result of which established that defendants facing the death penalty are constitutionally entitled to court-appointed counsel if they cannot afford one, and the right to effective representation.

Slave Codes of Georgia Sometimes called "black codes," these were laws passed by Georgia and other Southern states after the Civil War to restrict the freedom of black people to be employed and paid a fair wage, to move, to own land and to testify in court. These were outlawed by the Fourteenth Amendment.

Swann v. Charlotte-Mecklenburg Board of Education Landmark decision by the United States Supreme Court in 1971 upholding the busing program intended to hasten the process of racial integration of public schools.

Thirteenth Amendment Amendment to the United States Constitution that ended slavery; ratified in December 1865.

white supremacy Racist ideology based on the belief that white people are superior to and should dominate all other races.

writ Written command by a legal authority to act, or stop acting, in some way.

Media Literacy Terms

"Media literacy" refers to the ability to access, understand, critically assess and create media. The following terms are important components of media literacy, and they will help you critically engage with the articles in this title.

angle The aspect of a news story on which a journalist focuses and develops.

attribution The method by which a source is identified or by which facts and information are assigned to the person who provided them.

balance Principle of journalism that both perspectives of an argument should be presented in a fair way.

chronological order Method of writing a story presenting the details of the story in the order in which they occurred.

commentary Type of story that is an expression of opinion on recent events by a journalist generally known as a commentator.

credibility The quality of being trustworthy and believable, said of a journalistic source.

critical review Type of story that describes an event or work of art, such as a theater performance, film, concert, book, restaurant, radio or television program, exhibition or musical piece, and offers critical assessment of its quality and reception.

editorial Article of opinion or interpretation.

feature story Article designed to entertain as well as to inform.

headline Type, usually 18 point or larger, used to introduce a story.

human interest story Type of story that focuses on individuals and how events or issues affect their lives, generally offering a sense of relatability to the reader.

impartiality Principle of journalism that a story should not reflect a journalist's bias and should contain balance.

intention The motive or reason behind something, such as the publication of a news story.

interview story Type of story in which the facts are gathered primarily by interviewing another person or persons.

motive The reason behind something, such as the publication of a news story or a source's perspective on an issue.

news story An article or style of expository writing that reports news, generally in a straightforward fashion and without editorial comment.

op-ed An opinion piece that reflects a prominent individual's opinion on a topic of interest.

paraphrase The summary of an individual's words, with attribution, rather than a direct quotation of their exact words.

quotation The use of an individual's exact words indicated by the use of quotation marks and proper attribution.

reliability The quality of being dependable and accurate, said of a journalistic source.

rhetorical device Technique in writing intending to persuade the reader or communicate a message from a certain perspective.

source The origin of the information reported in journalism.

style A distinctive use of language in writing or speech; also a news or publishing organization's rules for consistent use of language with regards to spelling, punctuation, typography and capitalization, usually regimented by a house style guide.

tone A manner of expression in writing or speech.

Media Literacy Questions

1. What type of story is "The Colored Race" (on page 12)? Identify how the writers' attitudes, tones and biases help convey their opinions on the topic.

2. Do you find the article "An Indian Encounter" (on page 16) to be credible? If so, in what ways? If not, why not?

3. Does Claude Sitton demonstrate the journalistic principle of impartiality in his article "Violence in Mississippi Has Roots in Slavery Furor of the 1830's; Racial Views Are Probably Unshaken" (on page 104). If so, how? If not, how could he have made his article more impartial?

4. What is the intention of the op-ed article "The Heartbeat of Racism Is Denial" (on page 196)? How effectively does Ibram X. Kendi achieve his intended purpose?

5. "Fifty Years of Crusading for the Negro in America" (on page 75) is an example of a critical review. What is the purpose of a critical review? Does this article achieve that purpose?

6. Compare the headlines of "The Conduct and Attitude of the Southern Opposition" (on page 42) and " 'I Have a Dream' " (on page 129). Which is a more compelling headline, and why? How could the less compelling headline be changed to better draw the reader's interest?

7. Is the article "Obama Elected President As Racial Barrier Falls" (on page 176) a commentary, news story or interview story? What elements of the article helped you draw your conclusion?

Citations

All citations in this list are formatted according to the Modern Language Association's (MLA) style guide.

BOOK CITATION

THE NEW YORK TIMES EDITORIAL STAFF. *Race Relations*. New York: New York Times Educational Publishing, 2019.

ARTICLE CITATIONS

THE CHARLESTON MERCURY. "The South and the Negro Vote." *The New York Times*, 30 March 1868, www.nytimes.com/1868/03/30/archives/the-south-and-the-negro-vote.html.

COOPER, MICHAEL. "Officers in Bronx Fire 41 Shots, And an Unarmed Man Is Killed." *The New York Times*, 5 Feb. 1999, www.nytimes.com/1999/02/05/nyregion/officers-in-bronx-fire-41-shots-and-an-unarmed-man-is-killed.html.

DAVIES, LAWRENCE E. "Upholds Japanese in Citizens' Right." *The New York Times*, 21 Feb. 1943, www.nytimes.com/1943/02/21/archives/upholds-japanese-in-citizens-right-federal-court-in-california.html.

DAVIS-DUBOIS, RACHEL. "New Racial Ideas Taught." *The New York Times*, 20 May 1934, www.nytimes.com/1934/05/20/archives/new-racial-ideas-taught-pupil-visits-and-programs-help-develop-an.html.

FINE, BENJAMIN. "Militia Sent to Little Rock; School Integration Put Off." *The New York Times*, 3 Sept. 1957, timesmachine.nytimes.com/timesmachine/1957/09/03/91163355.html.

FRASER, C. GERALD. "Desegregation Course Charted By Legal Unit After Bus Ruling." *The New York Times*, 23 April 1971, timesmachine.nytimes.com/timesmachine/1971/04/23/81880115.html.

GONZALEZ, DAVID. "For Puerto Ricans, Sotomayor's Success Stirs Pride." *The New York Times*, 6 Aug. 2009, www.nytimes.com/2009/08/07/nyregion/07puerto.html.

GRAHAM, FRED P. "Marriage Curbs By States Scored." *The New York Times*, 11 April 1967, timesmachine.nytimes.com/timesmachine/1967/04/11/ 83587037.html.

HAYNES, GEORGE EDMOND. "Move to Curb Racial Strife." *The New York Times*, 20 Aug. 1943, timesmachine.nytimes.com/timesmachine/1943/08/20/ 85077008.html.

JONES, LOMBARD C. "Fifty Years of Crusading for the Negro in America." *The New York Times*, 22 Dec. 1940, www.nytimes.com/1940/12/22/archives/fifty -years-of-crusading-for-the-negro-in-america.html.

KENDI, IBRAM X. "The Heartbeat of Racism Is Denial." *The New York Times*, 13 Jan. 2018, www.nytimes.com/2018/01/13/opinion/sunday/heartbeat-of -racism-denial.html.

KING, JOHN E. "Texas Fights Bias to Insure Supply of Mexican Labor." *The New York Times*, 4 July 1948, timesmachine.nytimes.com/timesmachine/1948/07/ 04/86747269.html.

KING, SETH S. "Slaying Recalls Series of Deaths That Have Marked Rights Fight." *The New York Times*, 5 April 1968, timesmachine.nytimes.com/times machine/1968/04/05/90666306.html.

MYDANS, SETH. "Los Angeles Policemen Acquitted in Taped Beating." *The New York Times*, 30 April 1992, www.nytimes.com/1992/04/30/us/the-police -verdict-los-angeles-policemen-acquitted-in-taped-beating.html.

MYDANS, SETH. "Officer Says Beaten Man Resisted." *The New York Times*, 31 March 1991, www.nytimes.com/1991/03/31/us/officer-says-beaten-man-resisted.html.

NAGOURNEY, ADAM. "Obama Elected President as Racial Barrier Falls." *The New York Times*, 5 Nov. 2008, www.nytimes.com/2008/11/05/us/politics/ 05elect.html.

NELSON, NICOLE D. "When Will Black Lives Matter in St. Louis?" *The New York Times*, 20 Sept. 2017, www.nytimes.com/2017/09/20/opinion/when-will -black-lives-matter-in-st-louis.html. "

THE NEW YORK TIMES. "An 'Aberration' or Police Business as Usual?" *The New York Times*, 10 March 1991, timesmachine.nytimes.com/timesmachine/ 1991/03/10/467091.html.

THE NEW YORK TIMES. "Arrest of a Fugitive Slave." *The New York Times*, 9 Dec. 1851, www.nytimes.com/1851/12/09/archives/arrest-of-a-fugitive-slave .html.

THE NEW YORK TIMES. "Bar Negro Women's Vote." *The New York Times*, 3 Nov. 1920, www.nytimes.com/1920/11/03/archives/bar-negro-womens-vote

-savannah-judges-refuse-their-vote-white-women.html.

THE NEW YORK TIMES. "Better Relations Between Races Sought At a Student Conference in the South." *The New York Times*, 20 July 1930, www.nytimes .com/1930/07/20/archives/better-relations-between-races-sought-at-a-student -conference-in.html.

THE NEW YORK TIMES. "The Chaplin Case." *The New York Times*, 24 Sept. 1851, www.nytimes.com/1851/09/24/archives/editorial-article-1-no-title.html.

THE NEW YORK TIMES. "Civil Rights Victory." *The New York Times*, 11 Feb. 1964, www.nytimes.com/1964/02/11/archives/civil-rights-victory.html.

THE NEW YORK TIMES. "The Colored Race." *The New York Times*, 24 Sept. 1851, timesmachine.nytimes.com/timesmachine/1851/09/27/87821894.html.

THE NEW YORK TIMES. "The Conduct and Attitude of the Southern Opposition." *The New York Times*, 11 Sept. 1868, www.nytimes.com/1868/09/11/archives/ the-conduct-and-attitude-of-the-southern-opposition.html.

THE NEW YORK TIMES. "The Consummation! Slavery Forever Dead in the United States." *The New York Times*, 19 Dec. 1865, www.nytimes.com/1865/12/19/ archives/the-consummation-slavery-forever-dead-in-the-united-states -official.html.

THE NEW YORK TIMES. "Decision of the Supreme Court in the Dred Scott Case — The Position of Slavery in the Constitution." *The New York Times*, 9 March 1857, www.nytimes.com/1857/03/09/archives/the-dred-scott-case-decision-of -the-supreme-court-in-the-dred-scott.html.

THE NEW YORK TIMES. "Douglas vs. Douglass, Settlement of Nebraska." *The New York Times*, 13 Oct. 1854, https://www.nytimes.com/1854/10/13/archives/ douglas-vs-douglass-settlement-of-nebraska.html.

THE NEW YORK TIMES. "Dr. King Deplores 'Long Cold Winter' On the Rights Front." *The New York Times*, 20 June 1967, www.nytimes.com/1967/06/20/ archives/dr-king-deplores-long-cold-winter-on-the-rights-front.html.

THE NEW YORK TIMES. "Emancipation. President Lincoln's Proclamation." *The New York Times*, 3 Jan. 1863, www.nytimes.com/1863/01/03/archives/ emancipation-president-lincolns-proclamation-the-slaves-in-arkansas.html.

THE NEW YORK TIMES. "The Ghetto Explodes in Another City." *The New York Times*, 16 July 1967, www.nytimes.com/1967/07/16/archives/race-relations -the-ghetto-explodes-in-another-city.html.

THE NEW YORK TIMES. "Housing Plan Sets Tenancy Standards." *The New York Times*, 2 Dec. 1945, timesmachine.nytimes.com/timesmachine/1945/12/02/ 113130277.html.

THE NEW YORK TIMES. "How to Prevent Riots." *The New York Times*, 17 Aug. 1943, www.nytimes.com/1943/08/17/archives/how-to-prevent-riots.html.

THE NEW YORK TIMES. "Incident at Selma." *The New York Times*, 9 March 1965, timesmachine.nytimes.com/timesmachine/1965/03/09/98455134.html.

THE NEW YORK TIMES. "An Indian Encounter." *The New York Times*, 22 Sept. 1851, www.nytimes.com/1851/09/22/archives/an-indian-encounter.html.

THE NEW YORK TIMES. "Is the Turk a White Man?" *The New York Times*, 30 Sept. 1909, www.nytimes.com/1909/09/30/archives/is-the-turk-a-white -man.html.

THE NEW YORK TIMES. "Letter of the Chinamen to his Excellency, Gov. Bigler." *The New York Times*, 5 June 1852, https://www.nytimes.com/1852/06/05/ archives/the-chinese-in-california-curious-document-letter-of-the-chinamen .html.

THE NEW YORK TIMES. "Louisiana's Separate Car Law." *The New York Times*, 19 May 1896, www.nytimes.com/1896/05/19/archives/louisianas-separate -car-law.html.

THE NEW YORK TIMES. "A Lynching in Brooklyn." *The New York Times*, 16 Dec. 2008, www.nytimes.com/2008/12/17/opinion/17wed3.html.

THE NEW YORK TIMES. "Negro Planning Jobless March." *The New York Times*, 25 Feb. 1963, timesmachine.nytimes.com/timesmachine/1963/02/25/102284477.html.

THE NEW YORK TIMES. "Negro Protests Lead to Store Closings." *The New York Times*, 7 Feb. 1960, www.nytimes.com/1960/02/07/archives/negro-protests -lead-to-store-closings.html.

THE NEW YORK TIMES. "Negroes' Boycott Cripples Bus Line." *The New York Times*, 6 Dec. 1955, www.nytimes.com/1956/01/08/archives/negroes-boycott -cripples-bus-line-carrier-in-montgomery-ala.html.

THE NEW YORK TIMES. "Negroes Mob Photo Play." *The New York Times*, 18 April 1915, www.nytimes.com/1915/04/18/archives/negroes-mob-photo-play -boston-police-clear-lobby-and-birth-of-a.html.

THE NEW YORK TIMES. "Plain Truths for the Negroes." *The New York Times*, 24 Sept. 1870, www.nytimes.com/1870/09/24/archives/plain-truths-for-the -negroes.html.

THE NEW YORK TIMES. "The President's Proclamation." *The New York Times*, 3 Jan. 1863, timesmachine.nytimes.com/timesmachine/1863/01/03/78700901 .html.

THE NEW YORK TIMES. "Race Problem Conference; Speakers at Montgomery Discuss Lynching — Extermination of Blacks Said to Be Inevitable." *The

New York Times, 11 May 1900, www.nytimes.com/1900/05/11/archives/race
-problem-conference-speakers-at-montgomery-discuss-lynching.html.

THE NEW YORK TIMES. "Racial Issues Stirred by Mississippi Killing." *The New
York Times*, 18 Sept. 1955, timesmachine.nytimes.com/timesmachine/1955/
09/18/91366170.html.

THE NEW YORK TIMES. "Socialist Advises Negroes to Strike; Speech by Clarence Darrow Stirs Sociologists in Cooper Union to Warm Protest." *The New
York Times*, 13 May 1910, www.nytimes.com/1910/05/13/archives/socialist
-advises-negroes-to-strike-speech-by-clarence-darrow-stirs.html.

THE NEW YORK TIMES. "Standing Up for Civil Rights." *The New York Times*, 23
March 1988, www.nytimes.com/1988/03/23/opinion/standing-up-for-civil
-rights.html.

THE NEW YORK TIMES. "West Coast Moves to Oust Japanese." *The New York
Times*, 29 Jan. 1942, timesmachine.nytimes.com/timesmachine/1942/01/29/
85020540.html.

THE NEW YORK TIMES. " 'Wetback' Patrol to Be Stepped Up; 500 Officers to
Augment Unit of 256 on Mexico Border to Halt Alien Influx." *The New York
Times*, 10 June 1954, https://www.nytimes.com/1954/06/10/archives/
wetback-patrol-to-be-stepped-up-500-officers-to-augment-unit-of-256.html.

THE NEW YORK TIMES. "What Next?" *The New York Times*, 22 Feb. 1870, www
.nytimes.com/1870/02/22/archives/what-next.html.

THE NEW YORK TIMES. "A Woman's Protest." *The New York Times*, 21 March
1915, www.nytimes.com/1915/03/21/archives/a-womans-protest-history
-distorted-for-purposes-of-a-moving-picture.html.

THE NEW YORK TIMES. "Woman's Rights and the Fashions — A Rebuke from
'Sojourner Truth.' " *The New York Times*, 3 Nov. 1870, https://www.nytimes
.com/1870/11/03/archives/womans-rights-and-the-fashionsa-rebuke-from
-sojourner-truth.html.

THE NEW YORK TIMES. "Written on the Screen." *The New York Times*, 28 Feb.
1915, www.nytimes.com/1915/02/28/archives/written-on-the-screen.html.

RESTON, JAMES. " 'I Have a Dream.' " *The New York Times*, 29 Aug. 1963,
timesmachine.nytimes.com/timesmachine/1963/08/29/89957613.html.

ROBINSON, LAYHMOND. "New York's Racial Unrest: Negroes' Anger Mounting."
The New York Times, 12 Aug. 1963, timesmachine.nytimes.com/
timesmachine/1963/08/12/81822935.html.

SAVAGE, CHARLIE. "Korematsu, Notorious Supreme Court Ruling on Japanese
Internment, Is Finally Tossed Out." *The New York Times*, 26 June 2018,

www.nytimes.com/2018/06/26/us/korematsu-supreme-court-ruling.html.

SCHEMO, DIANA JEAN. "U.S. Schools Turn More Segregated, a Study Finds." *The New York Times*, 20 July 2001, www.nytimes.com/2001/07/20/us/us -schools-turn-more-segregated-a-study-finds.html.

SCHMITT, ERIC. "Broader Palette Allows for Subtler Census Portrait." *The New York Times*, 12 March 2001, https://www.nytimes.com/2001/03/12/us/ broader-palette-allows-for-subtler-census-portrait.html.

SENGUPTA, SOMINI. "Sept. 11 Attack Narrows the Racial Divide." *The New York Times*, 10 Oct. 2001, www.nytimes.com/2001/10/10/nyregion/a-nation -challenged-relations-sept-11-attack-narrows-the-racial-divide.html.

SITTON, CLAUDE. "Birmingham Bomb Kills 4 Negro Girls in Church; Riots Flare; 2 Boys Slain." *The New York Times*, 16 Sept. 1963, www.nytimes.com/1963/ 09/16/archives/birmingham-bomb-kills-4-negro-girls-in-church-riots-flare -2-boys.html.

SITTON, CLAUDE. "Negro Rejected at Mississippi U.; U.S. Seeks Writs." *The New York Times*, 21 Sept. 1962, www.nytimes.com/1962/09/21/archives/ negro-rejected-at-mississippi-u-us-seeks-writs-3-educators-face.html.

SITTON, CLAUDE. "Violence in Mississippi Has Roots in Slavery Furor of the 1830's; Racial Views Are Probably Unshaken." *The New York Times*, 3 Oct. 1962, timesmachine.nytimes.com/timesmachine/1962/10/03/90196869.html.

STREATOR, GEORGE. "Big Negro Colonies Worry West-Coast." *The New York Times*, 4 May 1947, www.nytimes.com/1947/05/04/archives/big-negro -colonies-worry-west-coast-san-francisco-bay-area-with.html.

TURKEWITZ, JULIE. "There's Never Been a Native American Congresswoman. That Could Change in 2018." *The New York Times*, 19 March 2018, www .nytimes.com/2018/03/19/us/native-american-woman-congress.html.

VEGA, TANZINA, AND JOHN ELIGON. "Deep Tensions Rise to Surface After Ferguson Shooting." *The New York Times*, 16 Aug. 2014, www.nytimes.com/ 2014/08/17/us/ferguson-mo-complex-racial-history-runs-deep-most-tensions -have-to-do-police-force.html.

Index

A

abolitionism, 10–11, 12,
  105, 197
American Council on Race
  Relations, 82, 84
American Federation of
  Labor, 110
American Indians, 16–17,
  200–204

B

Baldwin, James, 132, 137
Black Lives Matter, 9,
  193–195
Black Muslims, 115, 122,
  127–128
Bloody Sunday in Selma,
  Ala., 138
Boilermakers International,
  83
boycotts, 93–94, 113, 120, 139
Brotherhood of Sleeping
  Car Porters, 110
Brown, Michael, 187–189,
  193

C

Chaney, James E., 145
Chinese immigrants,
  18–24, 47–48
Civil Rights Act of 1963,
  137
Civil Rights Project, 169,
  170
Civil Rights Restoration
  Act, 150

Civil War, 42–45, 64, 105
Cold War and protest
  movement, 121
Communist Party, 78, 91,
  107–108, 117
Congress of Racial Equality
  (CORE), 117, 124, 125,
  126–127
Cooper, Michael, 161–164
Crisis, The, 77

D

Danials, Jonathn Myrick,
  146
Darrow, Clarence, 59–63
Davies, Lawrence E.,
  72–74
denial of racism, 196–199
desegregation, 107. See
  also integration
Diallo, Amadou, 161–164
discrimination. See also
  desegregation
  Civil Rights Act of 1963,
    137
  Civil Rights Restoration
    Act, 150
  housing, 118–121, 123, 126,
    141, 167, 169
  jobs, 139
  Mexican workers, 85–86
  protest movement,
    113–128
  Puerto Ricans, 184
  unions and seniority
    system, 83, 112

Dixon, Thomas, 64
Douglas, Arnold, 25–29
Douglass, Frederick, 25–29
Dred Scott decision, 30–31,
  42–43, 207
Du Bois, W. E. B., 75–78
Dunne, John R., 155

E

education
  dropout rate in New
    York, 119–120
  Du Bois and Washington,
    differing views on,
    76–77
  standardized testing, 170
  test of citizenship, 47
Eligon, John, 187–192
Emancipation Proclama-
  tion, 32–34, 35–38
Emigrants Aid Societies,
  27
Evers, Medgar W., 145

F

Farmer, James, 117, 125
Ferguson, Missouri,
  187–192, 193–195
Fifteenth Amendment,
  46–48, 56
Fine, Benjamin, 95–98
Flanagan, Peggy, 204
48-hour rule, for police
  officers, 164
Fourteenth Amendment,
  42–45

Fraser, C. Gerald, 147-149
free blacks, 13, 25-29, 53
fugitive slaves, 15, 53, 55

G

Garrison, William Lloyd, 197
Garvey, Marcus, 122
Giuliani, Rudolph W., 164,
171
Gold Rush and Chinese
miners, 18-24
Gonzalez, David, 183-186
Goodman, Andrew, 145
Griffiths, D. W., 64
Grove City College case,
150

H

Henry, W., 15
high schools, and improv-
ing race relations, 69-71
housing discrimination,
82, 118-121, 123, 126, 141,
167, 169

I

immigration, illegal, at
Mexican border, 87
industrial education, 56,
59, 62
integration. See also
desegregation
Little Rock, Ark., schools,
95-98
protest movement,
123-124
resistance to, 104-109
in shipbuilding industry, 83
internment camps for
Japanese-Americans,
72, 205-209

J

Japanese-Americans,
72-74, 205-209

Jim Crow, 75, 77
jobs, 117, 126-127, 201-202.
See also unions
Jones, Lombard C., 75-78

K

Kansas, and question of
slavery, 25-29
Kendi, Ibram X., 196-199
Kennedy, John F., 123, 131,
132, 135, 137
Kennedy administration,
100, 112
King, John E., 85-86
King, Martin Luther, Jr.,
129-132, 135, 139, 145,
199
King, Rodney Glen,
151-160
King, Seth S., 145-146
Kress, S. H., and lunch
counter protests, 99
Kujabi, Momodou, 163
Ku Klux Klan, 65

L

labor
basis of slavery, 62
integration, in shipbuilding industry, 83-84
Mexican, in Texas, 85-86
Lincoln, Abraham, 32-34,
35
Little Rock High School,
95-98
Liuzzo, Viola Gregg, 146
Lucero, Marcelo, 182
lunch counter protests, 99
lynching
discussion of, 55-56
NAACP and fight against,
77-78
trial of murderers of
Emmett Till, 88-92

M

Malcolm X, 116, 122,
145-146
March on Washington, 129
marriage, interracial, in
Virginia, 143-144
McCain, John, 176-177,
179-181
Meredith, James H.,
100-103, 108, 146
#MeToo movement, 200
Mexican immigrants,
85-86, 198
Montgomery bus boycott,
93-94
Moore, William L., 145
Morrisroe, Richard F., 146
multiracial choices, in U.S.
Census, 165-168
Muslim Americans
post-9/11 New York,
171-173
travel ban, 205-208
Mydans, Seth, 153-160

N

Nagourney, Adam, 176-181
National Association
for the Advancement
of Colored People
(NAACP), 77, 83, 91,
97, 122
Native Americans. See
American Indians
naturalization, conflicts
of, 47
Nelson, Nicole D., 193-195
New York City
protest movement, 1960s,
113-128
unity, post 9/11, 171-175
Niagara Movement, 77
Nielson, William Allen, 79
nonviolence, 124, 193-195

O

Obama, Barack, 176–181, 184

occupancy standards and lack of housing, 82

P

Pan-African Congress, 77

Parks, Rosa, 93–94

Plessy vs. Ferguson, 53

poll tax, 46–47

Popham, John N., 88–92

Poughkeepsie Convention, 49–51

property values, 82

protest movement, 113–128

public housing, 83–84

public school classrooms, 169–170

Puerto Ricans
  contributions to New York, 184–186
  protest movement, 127
  Sonia Sotomayor's appointment, 183–186

Q

quota system for employment, 126–127

R

race relations
  church movement to promote, 80–81
  denial of racism, 196–199
  with police in Ferguson, Mo., 187–195
  post-9/11 New York, 171–175

racial profiling, 171, 190

Randolph, A. Philip, 110–112, 117–118, 120, 123, 124

Reconstruction, 42–48

religion
  and citizenship, 47
  leaders, and protest movement, 125

ordination, higher standards of, 54–55

Reston, James, 129–132

riots
  after Birmingham bombing, 133
  in Ferguson, Mo., 187–189
  in Los Angeles, after Rodney King verdict, 154–157
  Newark, N.J., 140–142
  prevention of, 79

Roberts, John G., Jr., 205, 208

Robinson, Layhmond, 113–128

Roosevelt, Franklin D.
  Japanese-American internment camps, 74, 207
  jobs for Negroes in defense industry, 112

S

San Francisco
  post-war migration of Negoes, 83–84

Savage, Charlie, 205–208

Schemo, Diana Jean, 169–170

Schmitt, Eric, 165–168

school integration
  Little Rock, Arkansas, 95–98

Schwerner, Michael H., 145

Scottsboro boys, 78

segregation
  of Mexican immigrants, 85–86
  Plessy vs. Ferguson, 53

pro-slavery views as basis, 105

return to, in classrooms, 169–170

Selma, Ala.
  Bloody Sunday, 138
  march, and subsequent murders, 146

Sengupta, Somini, 171–175

separatism and protest movement, 122–123

Service Bureau for Education in Human Relations, 69

Seward, William H., 38–39

Sitton, Claude, 100–109, 133–136

Slave Codes ("black codes"), 42–45

slavers
  compensating, for loss of slaves, 13–14

slavery. See also Reconstruction
  abolitionism, 10–11
  Emancipation Proclamation, 32–37
  property laws, in support of, 10, 12–14
  Thirteenth Amendment, 38–39

social equality
  Clarence Darrow's comments on, 62
  and former slaves, 49–51, 55
  poor whites versus freed slaves, 55

soldiers, Negro, in World War I, 77

Sotomayor, Sonia
  dissent of ruling on Trump v. Hawaii, 205–208

and Puerto Rican com-
munity, 183–186
states' rights, 104, 107
Streator, George, 83–84
students
relations between white
and Negro, 68
school segregation,
95–98, 169–170
special programs in N.J.
high schools, 69–71
Sucuzhañay, José, 182
Supreme Court
citizenship of Japanese-
Americans, 73–74
Dred Scott Case, 30–31
interracial marriage
laws, 143–144
Korematsu ruling over-
turned, 205–208
Plessy vs. Ferguson, 53
Swann et al. v. Charlotte-
Mecklenburg Board of
Education et al., 148

T
Thirteenth Amendment,
38–39

Till, Emmett, 88–92
Trotter, W. Munroe, 66
Truman, Harry S., 112
Trump, Donald, 196–199,
201–202, 205–208
Truth, Sojourner, 52
Turkewitz, Julie, 200–204
Turks and naturalization,
57–58

U
unemployment
plans for March on Wash-
ington, 110
rates of, among Negroes,
110, 118
unions, 81, 83, 110, 111, 112,
120, 123, 127
United African Nationalist
Movement, 128
University of Mississippi
and integration, 104–109
Urban League, 83–84
U.S. Census and broad-
ened racial categories
choices, 165–168

V
Vega, Tanzina, 187–192

voting rights
barring Negro women, 67
Civil Rights Act of 1963,
137
former slaves, 45–46
turnout for Obama,
180–181

W
Wallace, George C., 133,
134, 138
Washington, Booker T., 76
Wells-Barnet, Ida, 60–61
White Citizens Councils,
97, 106, 143
white flight, 82, 187–190
white supremacy, 90,
105–106, 198
women
in politics, 186, 201–204
voting rights, 52, 67
Woolworth, P. W., protests,
99